Journey to Jerusalem

The Story of One Messianic Jewish Family's Struggle to Make Aliyah

(immigrate to the land of Israel)

by

Hannah Nesher

Scripture quotations are taken from the Hebrew-English Bible. Copyright © by Bible Society in Israel 1996 and the Israel Association for the Dissemination of Biblical Writings. The Bible Society in Israel, P.O. Box 44 Jerusalem, 91000 Israel

Scripture quotations taken from the HOLY BIBLE, NEW INTERNATIONAL VERSION. Copyright © 1973, 1978, 1984 by International Bible Society. Used by permission of Zondervan Publishing House.

ISBN# 978-0-9733892-8-9

For speaking engagements please contact Hannah:

> Hannah Nesher, Voice for Israel
> Suite #313- 11215 Jasper Ave.
> Edmonton, Alberta
> T5K 0L5 Canada

www.voiceforisrael.net

Copyright © 2008 by Voice for Israel

All rights reserved under International Copyright Law. Contents and/or cover may not be reproduced in whole or in part in any form without the express written consent of the Publisher.

Cover design by James Vanderwekken - jvnderwe@hotmail.com

DEDICATION

To the God of my fathers, Avraham, Yitzchak and Yaacov,

יהוה

אהיה אשר אהיה

To You whose name says

You will be whoever You will be –

Thanks for being all I have ever needed!

And to Your Son and Messiah Y'shuah

ישוע

For your obedience to the Father

For being led like a lamb to the slaughter

For pouring out your soul unto death

So that I could live!

A Special Thank You

I would like to say *todah rabah* (thanks very much) and publicly acknowledge my debt of gratitude towards some of the many people who helped with this work.

First of all, to my mother and father who gave me life. Thank you for your courage in training up this daughter of yours through all our ups and downs. Although we may not always agree on theology, your love has remained constant.

To David, for applying your excellent technical skills to help bring this book to publication. Thank you for your love, encouragment and steadfast faith - and for the gift of our two wonderful children.

To my children, Clayton, Courtney, Timothy, Liat, and Avi-ad, who each supplied material and inspiration for my writing. Thanks for your patience with the crazy times in our family - for loving and forgiving me. Big hugs to Clayton for his great technical support.

To our ministry partners for your faithful love, fervent prayers and generous support. May you be fully rewarded by the God of Israel under whose wings you have taken refuge - Ruth 2:12

To James Vanderwekken for his awesome graphic design work and technical support. You are a treasure!

To Denis Vanderwekken & his late wife, Corrie for their friendship, support, and help in the journey. Corrie - I miss you!
To Marilyn for your intercession & willingness to proofread.

Most of all, to the Holy Spirit (Ruach Hakodesh), for giving me the inspiration, motivation, and words to write.

Todah rabah! (thanks so much!) תודה רבה

Contents

PART ONE: EVERYTHING YOU ALWAYS WANTED TO KNOW ABOUT ALIYAH

Introduction: Passover and the Three Sons..................9

Why Another Book About Israel?..................13
A Dark Night of the Soul..................15
Direction from the Lord..................21
Mount Gilboa..................23
Get Up Off Your Face..................25

1 **Aliyah - Going Up to the Land**..................28
Beware the Spies..................28
So You Want to Make Aliyah..................29
The 'How' of Aliyah..................31
To Convert or not to Convert?..................35
Dreams of Messiah..................38
Next Year in Jerusalem..................38
The Ingathering of the Exiles..................41

2 **Restoration of the Land**..................44
Desert Transformed into a Garden of Eden..................44
Mountain of Death..................46
Partnership Between God and Man..................47
Tu Bishvat..................51
Land of Milk and Honey..................56
Marvels and Wonders..................58

3	**Our Personal Exodus**...**59**
	Emanuel - God With Us...63
	Bringing Back the Captives...65
	They Went Not Knowing
	Where They Were Going...65
	Divine Guidance...68
	The Battle for the Land...70

4	**Facing the Giants in the Land**...**80**
	Christians for Israel...82
	Putting Down Roots...84
	A Better Place Prepared for Us...95
	Childbirth in Israel...97
	The Educational Giant...103

5	**Journey to Jerusalem**...**106**
	Moving Under the Cloud...106
	Renting in Israel...107
	A Divine Appointment...110
	Welcome to the Family...113
	Love at First Sight...115
	Voice of the Bride and the Bridegroom...119

6	**God's Plan for the Jewish People in the Diaspora: To Come Home**...**122**
	An Urgent Appeal for Aliyah...122
	The Commandment to Live in the Land...128
	You Can Catch More Bees with Honey...132

7	**God's Plan for Israel: Our God Will Save Us!**...**134**
	Spiritual Salvation...138
	The Sin of Achan...139
	Covenants - Blessing and Cursing...141

Changing the Locks..................141
For Us Or Against Us?..................143
Building Collapse..................143
False Covenants..................148
Covenants and Boundaries..................149
An Israeli State in Jordan?..................150
Painful Briers and Thorns..................151
Spiritual Warfare..................152
Everlasting Covenant..................153

8 **God's Plan for the Nations:**
Destruction of Israel's Enemies..................157
The Spirit of Korach..................158
The Spirit of Jezebel..................160
Vengeance for Zion's Sake..................161

9 **God's Plan for the Church:**
To Unify With Israel..................166
Grabbing Hold of the Jew..................167
A Note to Non-Jewish Believers..................169
Restoration of Both Houses of Israel..................170
God of Mercy..................174
Spiritual Restoration..................177
Spiritual Opposition..................181
Zeal for the Lord..................181
Stand Firm..................184
Larboring in the Harvest Fields..................185

Only in Israel - The Bloopers..................187

Postscript (March 24th, 2008)..................217
Cracks in the Foundation..................218
Back to Exile..................230
Up to the Northern Galilee..................233

PART ONE

EVERYTHING YOU ALWAYS WANTED TO KNOW ABOUT ALIYAH

But were afraid (or didn't know) to ask....

Introduction: Passover and the Three Sons

In the readings during the Pesach (Passover) seder[1] the rabbis tell a tale about three sons – one good and smart son who knew all the answers, one bad and wicked son who didn't care to know, and one simple, but ignorant son who didn't even know the questions to ask. This book is written for us simple people, who want to obey the call of God to make Aliyah (immigrate to Israel), but don't even know where to begin. It is also written for those lovers of Israel, Christian Zionists, who want to come to a better understanding of the plight of Messianic Jews whose desire is to 'come home'. Hopefully you will come to this place of understanding and connection through reading about our antics. In coming home, we made many blunders – some with humorous consequences, and some not so easy to laugh about, even

---

1 A Passover Seder is the traditional ritual meal used to celebrate Israel's Exodus from Egypt.

now. But through it all, God has been faithful; our story is a testimony to God's grace.

I once watched a Disney movie about Goofy competing in a race. Poor Goofy bumbled and fumbled his way through the entire obstacle course, making every mistake possible. But somehow, despite his ineptitude, he came up the winner holding the gold trophy. Such it so often seems with us; we are called to run the race set before us – to obey and follow the call of God on our lives - and yet we seem to fumble the ball every time. But it is God that gives us the victory in the end and causes us to triumph through His Messiah, Yeshua![2] And so this book is not written in order that someone may have the perfect Aliyah experience and make no mistakes, but just to perhaps prepare the way a bit – to smooth over some of the potential rocky places and help avoid some of the sand traps.

Everyone must come to Israel with his or her own personal scripture. This was ours and I give it to you in your journey to fulfill your destiny:

> **"Be strong and of good courage; do not be afraid, nor be dismayed, for the Lord your God is with you wherever you go."**
> (Josh. 1:9)

You Didn't Ask...!

I especially remember one particularly frustrating encounter. Had I, at the time, known that such experiences were to be fairly typical of daily life in Israel, we may not have attempted the Herculean effort of making aliyah as

---

[2] Yeshua is the Hebrew name for Jesus. It means God saves or salvation.

Introduction

Messianic Jews from a North American country. We were sitting in the absorption office in Petach Tikvah. The local office in Ariel had insisted that we make the journey to their larger branch office (for some unknown reason). Buses in Israel cause me to feel sick to my stomach at the best of times; and my condition of being five months pregnant at the time didn't help matters either. But if we have to we have to, so we endured the hour and a half bus ride up and down the mountains, in and out of barbed wire enclosed settlements. Finally we found the office...waited a couple more hours for our number to be called...met with the absorption counselor...she sent us back to Ariel. Why? We didn't know and couldn't find out. There, we would have to wait for the one day a week that the local office opened. Finally the day arrived. We waited another couple of hours until they called our number - again...met with the absorption counselor – again. Here, the clerk dutifully informed us that we didn't get the right papers in Petach Tikvah and would have to return there to obtain the correct forms. Now I was starting to lose my cool. *"Why were we not given the right papers in Petach Tikvah?"*, I demanded to know. *"You didn't ask!!"*, was her straight faced reply.

I hope that this book will help answer some of the questions about Israel that you didn't even know to ask. Thank you for the privilege of sharing the story of our journey to Jerusalem, a testimony of the amazing grace of the God of Israel.

> **"And see, now I go bound in the spirit to Jerusalem, not knowing the things that will happen to me there, except that the Holy Spirit testifies in every city, saying that chains and tribulations await me. But none of these things move me, nor do I count my life dear to myself, <u>so that I may finish my race with</u>**

joy, and the ministry which I received from the Lord Yeshua, to testify to the gospel of the grace of God." (Acts 20:22-24)

WHY ANOTHER BOOK ABOUT ISRAEL?

The earnest and sincere looking man challenged me with this straightforward question. Jim and Olga had driven from the Christian Embassy in Jerusalem to the settlement of Ariel to ask us about our situation as Jewish believers in Yeshua, attempting (with great difficulty) to 'make Aliyah'. Aliyah means literally to 'go up,' to immigrate to the land of Israel. This is what we believed God had called us to do – to leave the land of our exile, Canada, and ascend to Zion, our ancient homeland. It sounded so easy in the Bible when Abraham did it. *'Lech lecha!'* God said to him – Go ye! (Gen.12:1) And so Abraham packed up and left home, family, friends, and country to go to a place that remained as yet unknown to him, but that God promised to show him. So too, we packed and left everything and everyone we loved, leaving behind all our 'earthly security' with a promise that God would also lead us to a place He had prepared for us. The Word He gave us was this, **"Behold, I send an Angel before you to keep you in the way and to bring you into the place which I have prepared."** (Ex. 23:20)

The difference, we soon discovered, is that Abraham did not have the Israeli Ministry of the Interior to deal with (called Mizrat Hapnim in Hebrew). Shas, the ultra-religious political party, controlled this arm of the multi-faceted bureaucracy of Israel (until the June 1999 election). Most of these religious zealots despise Messianic Jewish believers, especially when they try to sneak into the country and 'steal Jewish souls' as they see it. This is what the Orthodox Jews consider happens when a fellow Jew is 'deceived' into accepting Yeshua as Messiah.

And so, we found ourselves homeless and practically destitute in Ariel, the capital of Biblical Samaria, (known in the media as the 'territories'), sitting atop the 'hills of Ephraim.' Because of the Ministry's stalling tactics and non-cooperation in granting us citizenship, we had lived in Israel for six months without the right to work, obtain medical insurance, or any of the benefits and assistance granted to new *olim* (immigrants). Many of these immigrants had flooded the country from the former Soviet Union in recent years, causing much friction with the native Israelis who question their 'Jewishness' and resent the preferential treatment they receive upon immigrating. Ironically, it was a Russian family who offered us a room in their house to live for the time being. God was faithful to provide through the generosity of His people. The Believers of Ariel took up an offering for us at Passover and presented it to us after we had enjoyed a *seder* (Passover meal) together – our first Passover in the Land. According to Jewish tradition, when we celebrate the Passover, we are to consider ourselves as if personally delivered out of slavery into freedom. As we drank the cups of wine, representing the promises of God to the nation of Israel, we especially praised Him for his promise to bring us into the Land of Israel.

> **"And I will bring you into the land which I swore to give to Avraham, Yitzchak, and Yaacov[3]; and I will give it to you as a heritage."** (Ex. 6:8)

---

3 Abraham, Isaac, and Jacob

God had fulfilled that promise in our lives that day. The body of Messiah in this community brought food parcels and lavished encouragement upon us, assuring us that they stood with us in this battle. The women pledged to fast and pray at least one day a week, specifically for our situation. Even the Daati (religiously observant Jews) of Ariel stepped in to help, whereas the secular would not. The rabbi presented us with a box containing all we would need to celebrate Passover – matzah, wine, grape juice, etc., as well as a food voucher for the neighborhood grocery store. One particular Daati family, my son's *gannenet* (kindergarten teacher) and her husband, took it upon themselves to try and find us an apartment – personally phoning and driving us to other settlements in search of a home. We felt we owed them, at least for the gas, but instead, they blessed us with *'tzedakah'* (charity) for Pesach. I came home and wept in gratitude, and in petition for their salvation.

Now the Christian Embassy, hearing of our plight, had been called in to help. We shared our hearts over steaming Russian tea and homemade Middle Eastern hummus and pita bread. When I confided in Jim that I was in the midst of writing a book about Israel, he looked at me with piercing eyes and asked, *'With all the books that have been written about Israel, what do you think you have to say that has not already been said?'* I was taken aback. He waited expectantly for an intelligent answer that I did not seem to possess. All I could say was, *'I believe God wants me to write it.'*

A Dark Night of the Soul

The question took me back to that fateful 'dark night of the soul,' when God confirmed to me that this book must be written. Our first months were spent living in the beautiful apartment of an American believer. She herself lived in the Old City of Jerusalem, but kept another apartment in Netanya, a beautiful coastal city, and felt led by the Holy Spirit, after hearing me share my testimony at a Pro-Life Conference,[4] to offer us rent-free accommodations for three whole months! Here, in December of 1998, together with all of our children, we celebrated the Feast of Chanukah, Festival of Lights, courage and Miracles.[5] For forty years, while playing a Chanukah dreidle[6] game, I had recited the familiar refrain, Nes Gadol Haya *Sham*, which is what we say in exile: A great miracle happened *there* (in Israel). How glorious to have the privilege of, for the first time, saying, "Nes Gadol Haya *Poh*" : A great miracle happened *here*! This free apartment was our first great miracle in the land – and it happened on our very first day, just hours after embarking from our El Al flight. In the beginning, the sun, sea, and surf seemed like paradise – too good to be true.

The honeymoon phase.

---

4 See DVD Because He Lives, Hannah's personal testimony, recorded at Be'ad Chaim (Pro-Life Israel) conference near Jerusalem. Testimony is also available as a book, Grafted In Again. Available by mail or through our website.

5 See Chanukah book and DVD; available by mail or through our website: www.voiceforisrael.com

6 Dreidle: a spinning top Jewish children play with on Chanukah

A dark-complexioned man named Sinai, whom we met riding his white horse on the Netanya beach, looking like he just stepped out of the movie, 'Arabian Nights' astride his white stallion, called living in Netanya a 'fairy tale.'

Riding a White Stallion on Netanya Beach.

Somewhere, however, this fairy tale turned sour. Instead of the 'happily ever after' ending, disappointment and discouragement set in as we became aware that the Ministry officials suspected my faith in Yeshua and therefore refused to grant us citizenship. Apparently, someone from our home town 'informed' on us, telling them that we are members of ' Jews for Jesus'. Although we are not 'card-carrying' members of this particular organization, the 'accusations' were true in the broad sense – we were and are disciples of Yeshua Hamashiach[7], the Jewish Messiah. In their understanding, Jews who believe in Jesus have converted to Christianity and therefore disqualify themselves from the right to live in the Land. For us, however, believing in and

---

7 Hamashiach – Hebrew word meaning 'the Messiah'.

following a Jewish Messiah has only made us even 'more Jewish' than before we came to faith. God has given us a new heart and a new spirit to now desire to live according to His commandments, rather than the secular, worldly lifestyle we lived before. Yeshua was 'the way' for us to re-connect with our Father, the God of Israel. We now only wanted to also re-connect with our people, Israel, and to live in the Land that God has promised us through our forefathers, Abraham, Isaac and Jacob.

After waiting for weeks and weeks, with high hopes and expectations, this negative answer from the ministry burst our bubble. An overwhelming sense of betrayal – "Who would have done such a thing? - combined with suffering a painful miscarriage at the same time, led to such pain and disappointment that it seemed beyond what I had the capacity to bear. Doubts tormented my mind with thoughts such as: "Had God really called us? Was he really with us? Had we 'missed God'? Why could I not hear His voice or sense His presence anymore?" I read the Word of God that said 'None would be barren in the Land..." and wondered then what was wrong with me? [8] Running all the way down the steps to the now deserted, winter beach, I fell upon the sand and wept: *"Eli! Eli! Lamah Azavtani" (My God, my God, why have you forsaken me?) (Psalm 22:1) Did you really bring us to this land, just to send us back into exile again in defeat?"*

Days blurred, one blending into the other, as we waited, waited, waited, trying to keep the children (and ourselves) occupied, contacting our fellowship group in Canada, pleading for their prayer support. My Israeli brother-in-law warned us not to visit any Messianic Congregations until we had our papers, but we became so lonely and desperate for the fellowship of the Body of Messiah that we did visit

---

8 Deut. 7:14

the kehilla[9] in Netanya. Coming from a democratic country where our human rights are zealously guarded, we could not believe that anyone would actually spy on us to track our whereabouts. We had a lot to learn about the zeal of anti-missionaries[10] who do everything in their power to keep Messianic Jewish Believers out of the country; or if they happen to sneak in, to evict them. We were shocked to witness religious Jewish anti-missionaries videotaping people going in and out of a Messianic bookstore in Tel Aviv and infuriated to hear of people being kicked unceremoniously out of the country when their faces were recognized on the videotapes by the Israeli Ministry of Interior. In time, we learned to be more careful. We also recognized the dilemma for Jewish Believers who are torn between witnessing openly of their faith in Yeshua and their desire to remain in the Land of Promise. We soon found out that 'hush hush' was often the operative word in this land.

By January of 1999, my teenage daughter, Courtney, starved for peer interaction, bloated with 'family togetherness time', and worried about the continuation of her schooling started the semester at an American program in a nearby boarding school. We missed her terribly. She had always been my 'right hand girl', helping me always cheerfully and without complaint. As a little girl, I used to sing to her, 'You are my sunshine...' and indeed, her light truly did shine wherever she went. During my period of convalescence after my miscarriage, it was Courtney who comforted me, sat next to my 'mat' on the floor, and brought me delicious meals and

---

9 Kehilla: congregation

10 Anti-Missionaries are a group of zealous, religious Jews who actively oppose & persecute Jewish Believers and Messianic Congregations. They are also active outside the land (ie. Jews for Judaism) to recruit Jewish Believers back into Rabbinical Judaism and to discredit Yeshua's claims of Messiahship. Some Christians are caught in their trap as well and end up falling away from their faith. See Falling Away, article, on website: www.voiceforisrael.com

steaming hot cups of tea. My world felt so empty and sad without her, but I felt that I had to let her go, as there seemed to be no other option for her education at this point. We had no idea that educating our children in Israel was going to be so tough. We came under a serious misconception that Israel would have all kinds of programs in place to integrate our English-speaking children. But although some programs had been developed to integrate Russian and East European Jews making aliyah, it seemed as if us North American Jews were on our own.

Besides the huge language barrier, we also found that bullying and violence continued to be a serious problem in most Israeli schools. Large classes of over forty children and lack of discipline led to behavior problems in the classroom that our children had no idea how to handle. Some of the things our children personally experienced were that of other children climbing out of class windows in the middle of a lesson, mercilessly teasing and tormenting new immigrant students, throwing a brick in the face of another student, repeated 'flashing' of private body parts, and students locking teachers out of classrooms or busting down doors. Screaming at everyone seemed the total norm. I have talked to Israeli adults who admit being traumatized by their school experience. And so, since we wanted her to learn Hebrew and to integrate into Israeli culture and society, sending Courtney to an Americanized boarding school seemed the only available option.

Financially, our nest egg, which had been supernaturally supplied in a day, and seemed enormous at the time, now looked merely modest and likely inadequate. It was quickly showing signs of wear and tear, as we needed to continually convert the American dollars we had saved into sheckels[11] in order to eat and live. Money, true to scripture,

---

11 Sheckel: Israeli monetary currency. At this time (2000), $1 USD converted to 4 sheckels. $1 Can. To 2.5 sheckels (sh'kalim in Hebrew for plural)

sprouts wings and flies away at a particularly quick pace in Israel. As someone once said, 'This is the land of milk and honey, but the honey is expensive and the milk quickly goes sour!' We had no idea that the cost of living in Israel could be so high. We hesitated to travel, which would have used up our resources at an even faster rate. And so we felt 'stuck'. We prayed and prayed and fasted, and prayed some more. Friends of ours sent us a card with a picture of kneepads. It said 'thought you might need these' for spending so much time on our knees seeking the Lord – seemingly to no avail. But God was faithfully working behind the scenes.

Direction from the Lord

The only positive direction we received was from some friends in Canada, who had recently taken a trip to the United States. They just 'happened' to tune into a radio talk show recording of an Orthodox Jewish woman living in Israel, speaking about the threat of the New Age Movement, especially to the Jewish people. My friends tracked down the talk show host for more information, but could only find out her first name, Hannah, and her e-mail address. They e-mailed this scant information to me with excitement, saying that they believed it was very important for some reason that I contact her. Taking their advice, I e-mailed her immediately, simply requesting additional information on New Age and Jewish people. When I didn't receive a reply, I left it at that and forgot all about it. The Lord, however, had other plans.

Every time I thought I had reached the end of my rope with our immovable mountain I found that I could still slip a couple of notches lower. Now in one of those pits of despair; my feet seemed firmly stuck in the miry clay. Our friends contacted us again, asking if we had heard from this woman

in Israel. I replied that I hadn't, and they said, *"We feel so strongly that you are to meet with her, that we will pay for a rental car for you to go and find her."*
I asked, *"Do you know her last name now?"*
"No."
"Do you have any idea where she lives?" I asked.
"We think it's somewhere around Nablus," they replied.
"Well, that gives me a lot to go on. What am I to do – drive around in a rental car in the vicinity of Nablus, an Arabic town, calling out the window one of the most common Hebrew names in Israel?"

They didn't have any suggestions, and so I hung up the phone and prayed. I thought I would check my e-mail one more time before going to bed and behold – a reply from Hannah, giving me her web site address! I immediately went to the site and couldn't believe what I was reading. This Orthodox Jewish woman had an article on the internet that explained much of what I had been learning and teaching about in Canada: the threat of the New Age Movement, the rise of the New World Order, the danger of anti-Semitism in our day arising out of a Christianity stripped of its Jewish roots.[12] At the end of the article were the author's full name, postal box number, and city – Ariel. I did not recognize the name, but the city seemed to ring a bell, only I was not sure why. The next morning, my husband and I called information, asking if they had a listing for this woman. They didn't. In a flash, everything connected in my mind. I suddenly remembered that five years ago, as a new Believer, I had received a newsletter from someone living in Ariel with this same first name, but a different last name. Could this Hannah that I had once corresponded with years ago and the Hannah on this radio talk show possibly be one and the

---

12 See DVD's Unity in the Messiah, Exploring the Jewish Roots of the Christian Faith, and book, Flee Babylon.

same? The chances of this seemed remote, but I directed my husband to ask for a listing for the last name of the Hannah that I knew. Sure enough, this Hannah was listed! Excitedly, feeling a bit like Sherlock Holmes solving a mystery, we dialed the number and asked the woman who answered,

"*Is this Hannah_____?*" (the one I was familiar with).

"*Yes*", she answered.

"*Is this also Hannah_____?*" (the author of the article and talk show guest).

"*Yes*", she answered guardedly.

Then I asked, "*Did you send out a newsletter about five years ago?*" Silence greeted me, followed by a tentative "*Yes, ...who is this?*"

As I explained who I was and how I had gotten in touch with her, it dawned on both of us that it must have been God to connect us and that we must meet as soon as possible. That week, we rented a car and drove to Ariel to meet with Hannah and her family, who live as Orthodox Jews in this large settlement, the capital of Biblical Samaria.

Mount Gilboa

Our family enjoyed Hannah's gracious hospitality[13] and even stayed overnight, since a furnished apartment 'just happened' to be available to rent that night for a reasonable price, directly upstairs from Hannah's apartment. Not receiving any great revelation of why the Lord had brought us together, we left the next morning, thanking them for their hospitality, and set off to find the place that God had prepared for us in the land of Israel. We drove fairly aimlessly all day, not receiving any sign of divine guidance or leading, but

---

13 We did not yet understand how many Christians come to Israel expecting to receive hospitality from Jewish Believers and how this can sometimes become an issue for those living in the Land.

determined to find 'the place'. I'm not sure if we expected an angel to appear and say to my husband, 'Move over', and take over the driver's seat or what, but whatever we were expecting, it didn't happen. The hour was getting late; the sky grew dark and still – nothing. I thought we should stop at the nearest town to stay overnight in a hostel. We phoned, but they were all booked for the night. My five year old son in the back seat was, by this time, crying for fries from McDonalds, which was nowhere in sight. He had not yet adjusted to the fact that we no longer lived in the land of 'drive thru junk food' every few blocks. We decided to drive to the next youth hostel, which on the map looked fairly close. We drove to the vicinity, asked for directions (an 'iffy' thing to do at the best of times in Israel) and were told to drive up to the top of the mountain where we would find a place to stay for the night. Up we drove…and drove… and drove, never reaching the top of the mountain. Finally, we gave up, parked the car along the side of the road, and resigned ourselves to sleep sitting up for the night in the car. If we hadn't both been so discouraged, (and quite petrified), we might have noticed the beautiful view of the valley from where we parked near the Jordanian border. We weren't sure what or who would do us in first – a wild animal, a terrorist, or the hand of God!

At one point in the middle of the night, an Israeli army jeep patrol drove by and stopped, the soldier peering into the car with a flashlight. Thinking we were lovers trying to find a little seclusion for our 'rendezvous', they quickly retreated and drove off before we recovered from our surprise enough to ask how far to the top of the mountain and whether or not we would find a place to lodge for the night. Our 'mountain-top experience' may seem amusing now, but at the time, we were definitely not laughing. I remembered vaguely that this mountain, Gilboa, was mentioned in the bible, and so I thought it must be of some wonderful, Biblical significance and that God would speak to us through this. Looking it up, I found that Mount Gilboa was the site of a terrible defeat where Saul and his sons, including Jonathan, were slain by the enemy. Great! We didn't need to be told in any clearer language that we were off on the wrong track. Now, whenever my husband wants to indicate that we are doing something 'in the flesh' he just calls it Gilboa and I immediately understand.

Get Up Off Your Face

Having nowhere else to go, we returned to the apartment in Netanya that now seemed almost like a prison. The three months we had been granted by our gracious sister in the Lord was at an end, and although we knew she would not throw us out on the street, we felt that to stay longer would be to take advantage of her generosity. The eagle was definitely pushing the eaglets out of the nest, but we weren't sure we could fly. And so, I did what I usually do when I need a place of refuge – I fled to the bathroom, locked the door, lay on the floor, and wept until I had no strength to weep any more. I cried out to God, *"Why, God? How long, O God? Will you forget me forever?"*

I heard in reply, *"What are you doing down there on your face? Get up! ! Why should I give you any further direction or instruction when you have not even started what I have already instructed you to do?"*

I knew immediately the nature of my disobedience. I had failed, during all this available time, even during my weeks of bed rest after the miscarriage, to begin writing the book the Lord had directed me to write. I had always somehow 'known' that I would write a book. In fact, at nine years old, I did succeed in writing a book about my passion at the time – tropical fish. But God had called me to write about more than just pretty fish. In 1997, at a Missions Fest conference, I was struck by the number of people who approached me, saying that they wanted to share about the Messiah with a Jewish relative or friend, but just didn't know how to go about it. They wished they had something to give them that would explain about Yeshua from a personal Messianic Jewish perspective. I went home that night convicted by the Holy Spirit that I must record my testimony on paper, along with some suggestions on answering Jewish objections to Yeshua. This I did, by the grace of God, in one night, bringing photocopies the next day to hand out to people who asked. What a labor of love and joy! One man who received a copy was the head of International Ministries to Israel in Winnipeg, Manitoba. He printed an edited version in his newsletter and I received a letter from an author, encouraging me to write a book that could be used as an evangelical tool for both Jews and Gentiles. He said, *"I believe I am only confirming what God has probably already directed you to do."* He was right.[14]

And then there is life - the tyranny of the urgent that always seems to crowd out the important things in life – like writing a book. Everything else seemed to take higher priority, and unless I discovered a way to live without sleeping, it seemed that I would never find the time to write. And always, a brassy, strident inner voice would say, *"Who do you think you are to think you could write anything that would prove worthwhile?"* My lack of confidence combined with practical difficulties resulted in the book never even being started, let alone completed. It took this amount of pressure – a Mount Gilboa experience – to cause me to come to my senses and take direction from the Holy Spirit seriously. And so – to answer the question, *"Why another book about Israel?"* – I could only answer, "...because I believe God told me to." This was confirmed when I found out that Hannah, the

---

14 This booklet is available as 'You Know my Heart' in Hebrew as well as English through our website: www.voiceforisrael.com

woman from Ariel that God connected me with is an editor. I called her and she graciously agreed to help edit the book and get it to print. My family and I immediately moved to Ariel into the apartment above Hannah's. Later, I found out to whom this apartment belongs – an author of a book about the Mountains of Israel[15] – and she wrote it in the very apartment to which the Lord led us. Praise God!

I offer this book then, to you, and for the glory of God, praying that the words it contains will not return void but will accomplish the purposes of the Almighty God of Israel. May it bear much fruit for the Kingdom of the Lord.

---

15 The Mountains of Israel, by Norma Archboldt

CHAPTER ONE

ALIYAH - GOING UP TO THE LAND

Beware the Spies

When people heard about our plans to make Aliyah (immigrate to the Land of Israel), the most common reaction, (even among those in the Church) was one of bewilderment. *"Why, for goodness sake, would you consider pulling such a stunt?"* After all, we had just gotten married and were trying to establish our newly formed blended family; we were fairly comfortable and relatively secure and stable financially. Our children were well established in schools and connected with their friends, cousins and grandparents; in fact all of our family resided in Canada. A home fellowship group we had started to teach Torah, Hebrew, dance and worship was growing and flourishing. The list of reasons why we shouldn't make Aliyah far outweighed any reasons in favor. One leader of a Christian ministry that ironically promotes Aliyah from the former Soviet Union and Eastern Europe, warned us against going. He told us that Messianic Believers are scrounging from garbage bins in Israel! We decided to look upon all these negative reports as if they were coming from the mouths of the spies sent to Canaan, whose condemning report about the land caused the rest of Israel to become discouraged. We knew the unfortunate fate of these spies who fell under the wrath of God for maligning His Land, and so we determined to be like Caleb and Joshua, believing in the promises of God despite all the negative report that the land 'eats up its inhabitants'. The following is an article I wrote for a messianic publication on the necessity of this 'Joshua and Caleb' mentality for a successful Aliyah.

SO YOU WANT TO MAKE ALIYAH...

So, you want to make Aliyah – (literally, 'to go up') – to immigrate to the land of Israel. Mazal tov! (Congratulations). You've heard the call of God to come home to the land promised to the descendants of Abraham, Isaac, and Jacob as an everlasting possession. It's a big decision. Reading about someone leaving his home and family to travel by faith, to the destination that God would show him is much easier than actually doing it. It requires much prayer, seeking the Lord for His will, wisdom, and timing. For a successful Aliyah, one must possess first and foremost, not money, not a job offer, nor even mastery of Hebrew, but a 'Caleb and Joshua spirit'. Just as Joshua and Caleb believed that with God's help, they could face the giants and experience victory, so must we have this kind of faith in order to enter the land. There are plenty of 'ten spies' out there who will cause you to lose heart if you listen to their negative reports about the land of Israel – that it devours its inhabitants. We received so many that we decided when we reached ten, that would be our signal to make the big move. We had one person tell us that Messianic Jewish believers are actually picking out of the garbage in Israel. We laughed when we later found out that yes, Believers pick out of the trash, but so do most Israelis. Not because they're starving, but because this seems to be the Israeli's unofficial 'Salvation Army' system. Whatever you don't need, you place beside the garbage bin as a signal that it's free for whoever needs it. We know one Believer who built an entire computer out of the garbage. Another whose entire home is furnished out of the same source...

I heard one American who had made Aliyah several years previously say, in response to my inquiry as to whether or not to make Aliyah as a single parent, *'You don't need a special call from God to make Aliyah. You need a special calling from God to remain in exile.'* Biblically, living outside of the 'Promised Land' was a sign of God's wrath upon Israel for their unrepentant sins. The Jewish people were never meant to find peace and security outside the land of Israel. This 'brother in the Lord' did add however, that it would be extremely difficult financially, to survive in Israel as a single parent and that the children would need an 'abba' there. He lightheartedly asked how fast I could find this 'abba'(daddy) Little did I know how quickly the Lord would find him and bless me with a wonderful husband whose heart's desire was also to live in the land of Israel. A husband, however, is not mandatory. I recently received a call from a single mother who made Aliyah on her own with two teenage daughters. Nothing is impossible with God. Although perhaps one does not need to hear the voice of God audibly command, 'lech lecha' (go!), it helps. In those moments of doubt and despair, a specific word from God can be the rock to which you cling, knowing that you know that you know that God has called you at this time to make Aliyah. To me, He gave the scripture,

> **"Be strong and courageous. Do not be terrified; do not be discouraged, for the Lord your God will be with you wherever you go."**
> (Josh. 1:9)

Hopefully, this column will help prepare you for the

exciting, but challenging process of making Aliyah to the land of Israel. In the next issue, we will discuss two basic ways of immigrating to Israel along with their pros and cons, especially for believers in Yeshua. Shalom!

The following is article #2 in the series on Aliyah:

THE 'HOW' OF ALIYAH

Once you have understood the 'why' and firmly decided upon the 'what', the next most important consideration is the 'how'. How does one go about making Aliyah – immigrating to the land of Israel? And what special 'giants' may the Jewish Believer in Yeshua face in the land? Under the law of return, anyone defined as Jewish has the right to return home to the land God promised our forefathers, Abraham, Isaac, and Jacob. Although this remains a divine, Biblical right, for any Jew, the State of Israel does not extend this right, politically or legally, to 'Messianic Jews'.

"When Believers of Jewish descent immigrate to this Land, the application form inquires about nationality and religion. Each applicant, including Jews who believe in Yeshua are expected to answer honestly about their identity. Typically, Messianic Jews believe the most truthful answer in their hearts is that they remain Jewish. This, however, conflicts with a Supreme Court decision (December 25, 1989), which states that Messianic Jews are not to be considered Jewish for the purpose of the Law of Return. Therefore, the potential exists to assert that all Messianic Jews who made application for citizenship during the last ten years made a false declaration when they stated that they are Jewish. Under this line of reasoning, therefore, the vast majority of all Messianic Jews who immigrated during the last decade are legally vulnerable to revocation

of citizenship and expulsion from Israel." [16]

As you can see from the above excerpt crossing the Jordan into the Promised Land for Messianic Jews is becoming more and more difficult. Aliyah can be made in two basic ways: from the country of origin or from within Israel.

In this article, I will briefly outline the pros and cons of each method. Making Aliyah from one's country of origin is by far the better option if at all possible. Most major North American Jewish communities employ a 'shaliach' (literally a 'sent one') whose purpose is to encourage and facilitate immigrating from the diaspora to Israel. The advantages of arranging your Aliyah from the place to which you have been exiled are:

- The issue of your "Jewishness" will already have been settled outside the country; therefore, you will receive your identity number (called a teudat zehut) at the Ben Gurion airport.
- Living arrangements will also be pre-arranged. You will likely be placed into an absorption centre upon arrival with other new immigrants where you will learn Hebrew in a school called an ulpan.
- Your flight will be paid for by the Jewish agency.
- You will be able to bring more of your belongings for a very reasonable rate on an El Al flight.

It sounds good, doesn't it? What are the disadvantages

---

[16] From the Messianic Action Committee Freedom Report No. 71 (February 7, 2000) Note: Recently (April 2008), the Israeli Supreme Court came to a landmark decision for Messianic Jews wanting to make aliyah. Those who are Jewish on their father's side (since according to Rabbinical ruling, Jewish identity is passed through the mother) are now eligible to make aliyah even if they are followers of Jesus (Yeshua).

then? Just one – you might not stand a chance if people in your local community know that you are a Believer in Yeshua. Usually some zealot considers it their 'religious duty' to 'enlighten' the shaliach as to your personal religious beliefs about the Messiah. One family of Believers who did make Aliyah through a shaliach were 'informed upon' just a week or so before they were due to leave. The travel arrangements had already been made and everything was in place when the shaliach confronted them. They explained their conviction that as Jews believing in a Jewish Messiah, they remain Jews and still desire to 'go home'. After a long pause, this Israeli representative of the Jewish Agency signed the final papers saying, *"I hope I'm not making a big mistake!"* This, however, was twenty years ago, before the term "Messianic Jew" was well known among Israeli authorities. Today is a different story. Unless you are an Orthodox religious Jew making Aliyah for religious reasons, (the long sidecurls and black garb is a dead giveaway), you are immediately suspected of being a Believer in Yeshua. After all, what secular Jew in their right mind would immigrate to this hot, struggling, war-torn nation from the comfort of their prosperous, secure North American existence, likened to the 'flesh pots of Egypt'?

The disadvantages of making Aliyah from within Israel (coming on a tourist visa and then applying for citizenship at the Ministry of Interior), are intimidating:

- The process may take months or even years; you must have funds to cover this indefinite period of waiting time.
- During this time, you may not legally work or receive national health care benefits.
- You must pay for your own airline tickets.
- You must arrange your own accommodations at your own expense.
- Living in Israel can be costly!
- The waiting can be very difficult and discouraging

- You will only be able to bring two suitcases each and it will be very expensive to ship your belongings later.
- With children, you can multiply all these trials many times over. They may not be able to attend a school until they receive their identity number.

Even considering all the disadvantages of making Aliyah from within Israel, if you are a well-known Messianic Believer, it may be your only option. While touring Yad Vashem, the Holocaust Memorial Museum in Jerusalem, I was particularly touched this time by authentic film footage of Holocaust survivors attempting to get into the newly born state of Israel despite the British quota on Jewish immigration into 'Palestine'. I witnessed the grief and rage of those who were caught on illegal boats and forcibly sent back into exile. Weeping, I watched men, women and children physically resist, clinging to the bars of the ship with all the strength remaining in their weakened bodies. I felt the Lord showing me that this is a picture of Messianic Jews trying to get into the land of Israel today, (or possibly in the future) despite the religious, political, and legal blockades. Although some may manage to sneak in, even illegally according to the law of return, many others are, unfortunately, forced back into exile. One such example, an elderly Canadian couple, left just last week. After waiting months for an answer from the Ministry of Interior (Mizrat Hap'nim), they were requested to submit a statement about their religious beliefs. Of course they could not deny Yeshua, and so, with heavy hearts, they returned to Canada.

Some take a kind of fatalistic attitude about this: *"If God wants someone to make Aliyah then they will make it. If they don't then God doesn't want them here; they don't belong."* But the issue is not so black and white. God is calling His people home; we can expect opposition to God's plan. In every battle, casualties are inevitable, and this includes spiritual battles! We must remember always that we wrestle not against flesh and blood, but against spiritual forces working against the purposes of God. Is it fair to exclude Messianic Jews from the land? Of course not, as even the Israeli public and media recognizes. Recently, a newspaper article came out charging the Israeli Ministry of Interior with racism, for their persecution against non-Jewish spouses of Israeli citizens. We need to remember, though, that many people of God in the Bible suffered unjust treatment by others. Joseph, thrown into a pit, sold into slavery by his own brothers, and tossed into a prison cell for a crime he didn't commit is just one. Was the treatment that Yeshua received fair? But he entrusted himself into the hands of the Just and Righteous One. If we walk in Yeshua's footsteps, then we must also expect to be hated, rejected and so suffer for His name's sake and for the gospel as we are being conformed into His image. Whether our Aliyah is successful or not, we must maintain Yeshua's attitude of humility, love and forgiveness, even towards our 'enemies'. Be strong and of good courage, for the Lord your God is with you!

The following is article #3 in the series on Aliyah:

TO CONVERT OR NOT TO CONVERT?

One of the more thorny issues that some Messianic Believers wanting to make Aliyah must confront is that of conversion. Many Jewish Believers have married Gentile Believers, since Yeshua has made the two one and destroyed the *machitzah*, the barrier, the dividing wall of hostility. (Eph. 2:14) To the Israeli Ministry of Interior, however, – and in fact to most of Israeli society – the issue of lineage is of vital significance. According to the Rabbinical ruling of the day, Jewish lineage is determined through the mother. As a result, The Law of Return, which states that every Jew has the right to come to the country of Israel as an immigrant (oleh) applies to "any person born of a Jewish mother or has become converted to Judaism and who is not a member of another religion." The right to immigrate also extends to the oleh's child, grandchild, and spouse.

This is the letter of the law, but in actuality, the Ministry of Interior, who is given the charge to administer these regulations, has the power to grant or deny the right of Aliyah to whomever they choose. Therefore, discrimination may exist against non-Jews in Israel. Perhaps this is understandable, considering the historical nature of the State of Israel, rising out of the ashes of the holocaust, and its primary purpose – to provide a safe haven for Jews of every nation to live free in our ancient homeland. Unfortunately, this noble ideal may cause the non-Jewish spouse to feel as if he or she is treated as a "second class citizen in a Jewish nation."

This brings us to a difficult question. Should the non-Jewish spouse go through a formal conversion process before making Aliyah? Of course I am generalizing, but my observation is that many (not all) Believers who go through a formal conversion to Judaism through the avenue of Orthodox Rabbinical Judaism become confused in their faith or even end up denying Yeshua.[17] When we willingly place ourselves under the spiritual authority of those who hate Yeshua, even if they do not require us to openly deny Him, the dual and conflicting allegiance may ultimately cost us dearly.

> **"For what shall it profit a man, if he shall gain the whole world and lose his own soul?"**
> (Mark 8:36)

---

17 Falling Away, in articles archives on website, describes our personal experience with conversion.

We must always base our identity, sense of worth and security on the solid foundation of the eternal love that the Lord has for us, not our ethnic or racial heritage. This will give us the strength to withstand any persecutions that come against us here in the Land.

This is a question that cannot be answered by anyone but the Holy Spirit. It requires much prayer and seeking the Lord for His individual plan for yourself and your family. Reform and Conservative conversions have just recently been recognized within Israel. Orthodox Rabbinical Judaism practiced in Israel today to a large extent hates Messianic Believers, and is not the Biblical form of Judaism we find in the torah.

A Note to Jewish Believers Wanting to Make Aliyah

The task ahead of you may not be easy. In fact it may be impossible. But as Believers in the God of Israel and our covenantal relationship with Him through His son, Yeshua the Messiah, we have hope. Nothing is impossible with our God. Then again, you may find that you encounter no trouble whatsoever. It is possible that God may have granted you a calling to remain in the Diaspora to accomplish His purposes there for the time being. We must always remember, as someone reminded me, our primary goal is always to become conformed into the image of His son, not to live in the Land of Israel. And so let this goal always remain before us as we run the race. May God be with you wherever you go, His Spirit guiding you always, and may His perfect will be done in your lives.

Dreams of Messiah

Perhaps it may help to understand the 'why' of Aliyah by regressing to the origin of the whole Zionist movement. Shortly after the age of twelve, a young man was visited by a dream. The Bible reveals that God has often communicated with man in dreams and visions: Daniel's visions and dreams about the Messiah, Pharaoh's dream about the fat cows and skinny cows, Joseph's dream about the bushels of wheat bowing down to him, and many other examples. In this young man's dream, the King Messiah came, a glorious and majestic old man, who took him in his arms and swept off with him on the wings of the wind. The Messiah encountered the figure of Moses, and called to him: *"It is for this child that I have prayed."*

But to the boy, he said: *"Go, and declare to the Jews that I shall come soon and perform great wonders and great deeds for my people and for the whole world."* [18]

This boy's name was Theodor Herzl. He grew to become the most prominent champion of the cause of Zionism. Hertzel helped birth the modern state of Israel with the word, *"If you will it, it is no dream."*

Next Year in Jerusalem

In 1948, the nation of Israel was reborn in a day, silencing all those who would falsely boast that *they* are the 'new Israel and, *"God is finished with Israel and the Jews."*

> "Who has heard such a thing? Who has seen such things? Shall the earth be made to give birth in one day? Or shall a nation be born

---

18 Anton Darms, 'The Jew Returns to Israel", (Zondervan Publishing House, Grand Rapids, Michigan, 1965, p. 23)

at once? For as soon as Zion was in labor, she gave birth to her children." (Is. 66:8)

The book of Revelation describes an enormous red dragon with seven heads poised in front of the woman who was about to give birth, so that he might devour her child the moment it was born. (Rev. 12:4) Seven Arabic nations converged upon the newborn nation of Israel to devour her as soon as she was born, but the Lord's will for her survival prevailed. For over two thousand years, every Passover Seder has concluded with the refrain - *'L'shana haba-ah b'Yerushalayim'* (Next year in Jerusalem). Since the time of her punishment, when God scattered Israel among the nations, the exiles have longed to return home to Zion.

> "**By the rivers of Babylon, there we sat down and we wept when we remembered Zion... How shall we sing the Lord's song in a foreign land? If I forget you, O Jerusalem, let my right hand forget its skill! If I do not remember you, let my tongue cling to the roof of my mouth – if I do not exalt Jerusalem above my chief joy.**" (Ps. 137:1, 4-6)

The Israeli national anthem, **Hatikvah** (The Hope) expresses both this longing and this hope:

> "As long as in a Jewish heart,
> the soul's stirring has not ceased.
> The eye for longing will not rest,
> until it gazes upon Zion in the East.
>
> Our ancient hope will not perish.
> Hope for two thousand years,
> to be a free nation in our land,
> Zion and Jerusalem at last."

With Fury Poured Out

Proverbs tell us that an unfulfilled longing causes one to become heartsick, but a longing fulfilled is sweet to the soul. (Prov. 13:19) For many Jewish people, their souls have been satisfied with the sweetness of their return to Zion. Many more still need to come home, especially from North America, where most of the Jewish people live in comfort, prosperity, and security. God promises that He will accomplish this task, even if it takes the hand of His fury over the nations in order to do so. Just as God brought His wrath upon Egypt in order to deliver His children from bondage and bring them back to the land of their fathers, so will He once again stretch out His mighty arm in order to bring the Jewish people out of exile. He will defeat all false gods of materialism and idolatry, establishing His supremacy over the earth. With fury and judgment poured out upon the Gentile nations will He bring His people home. Then all shall know that He alone is Adonai, the Lord. This is His sworn oath!

> "What you have in your mind shall never be, when you say, 'We will be like the Gentiles, like the families in other countries, serving wood and stone.' 'As I live,' says the Lord God, 'surely with a mighty hand, with an outstretched arm, and <u>with fury poured out,</u> I will rule over you. I will bring you out from the peoples and gather you out of the countries where you are scattered, <u>with a mighty hand, with an outstretched arm, and with fury poured out.</u>'" (Ezek. 20:32-34)

These words are the exact same ones used in the vocabulary of the Exodus from Egypt, God's pouring out His wrath upon Pharaoh and the Egyptians with the Ten Plagues. This prophecy, however, is for sometimes in the future, when God will no longer be called the God who brought His people out of Egypt, but God who brought His people out of the countries of the North, and from all the places to which He scattered them. 'And they shall dwell in their own land." (Jer. 23:7-8)

The Ingathering of the Exiles

As part of His plan to restore Israel, God promises to bring back His people from even the most distant lands and from the uttermost parts of the earth:

> **"Even if you have been banished to the most distant land under the heavens, from there the Lord your God will gather you and bring you back. He will bring you to the land that belonged to your fathers, and you will take possession of it...The Lord your God will circumcise your hearts and the hearts of your descendants, so that you may love him with all your heart and with all your soul, and live."** (Deut. 30:4-6)

Notice that the return of the people to the land occurs before their spiritual awakening, not after. They return to the land first and then to the Lord. Most of those returning are doing so in unbelief with regards to their Messiah, many are atheists or agnostic but this is also in God's perfect plan. Once the exiles of Israel are safely restored to live in the land belonging to their fathers, then the Lord will perform the 'bris'[19], the circumcision of their hearts.

> **For I will take you from among the nations, gather you out of all countries, and bring**

---

19 Bris is short for Brit Millah, the cutting of the covenant with every 8 day old male infant through circumcision.

you into your own land. *Then* **I will sprinkle clean water on you, and you shall be clean; I will cleanse you from all your filthiness and from all your idols.** (Ezekiel 36:24-25)

The cities and towns of Israel are truly being re-built and inhabited by the descendants of Abraham, Isaac, and Jacob. People are planting gardens and enjoying the fruit off their own trees in the land. This year, we enjoyed grapes off the vine, apricots, avocados, lemons, peaches, pomegranates, persimmons, pears and almonds – all off the trees in our back yard. I often sit and read under the shade of our fig tree.

"And I will bring again the captivity of my people Israel, and they shall build the waste cities, and inhabit them: and they shall plant vineyards, and drink the wine thereof; they shall also make gardens, and eat the fruit of them." (Amos 9:14)

Each day as I walk along the streets of this Israeli village, I greet the elderly Russian immigrants, sitting on the benches with their canes, enjoying the sunshine and exchanging daily gossip.

"Thus says the Lord of hosts: 'Old men and old women shall again sit in the streets of Jerusalem, each one with his staff in his hand because of great age." (Zech. 8:4)

It fills my heart with joy to see my little boy, Shmuel, playing 'cadoor regel' (soccer) outside with the other 'Israeli' boys. On Yom Kippur (The Day of Atonement) even the most secular Jews dare not drive their cars on this most Holy of Holy days; therefore the streets are deserted of any motorized vehicles. This year, the neighbor girls invited Shmuel to join them in their annual Yom Kippur rollerblading and bike riding up and down the streets. I stood in awe at witnessing the very fulfillment of ancient Hebrew prophecies regarding this land.

> **"The streets of the city shall be full of boys and girls playing in its streets."** (Zech. 8:5)

Before my very eyes, both old and young unknowingly take part in fulfilling ancient prophecy. What a privilege to be part of the generation witnessing the national restoration of Israel.

Children playing in the streets.

CHAPTER TWO

RESTORATION OF THE LAND

Desert Transformed into a Garden of Eden

God commands the prophet Ezekiel to prophesy, not only to the people, but also to the land itself – to the mountains and hills, to the ravines and valleys:

> "But you, O mountains of Israel, will produce branches and fruit for my people Israel, for they will soon come home." (Ezek. 36:8)

God restored the fruitfulness of the land in preparation for the return of His people Israel. Here, what once used to be desert wastelands are now blooming and being transformed into the most glorious gardens, full of orchids and flowers of all colors of the rainbow. Truly, places in Israel must resemble the Garden of Eden in its beauty, as prophesied.

> "For יהוה will comfort Zion, He will comfort all her waste places; He will make her barren wilderness blossom like Eden, and her desert like the garden of Yehovah; joy and gladness shall be found therein, thanksgiving, and the voice of melody." (Is. 51:3)

This ecological miracle foreshadows the wonderful restorative work the Lord will accomplish in creating the new heavens and new earth following its end time devastation.

> "Behold, I will create new heavens and a new earth...for I will create Jerusalem to be a delight and its people a joy. I will rejoice over Jerusalem and take delight in my people; the sound of weeping and of crying will be heard in it no more." (Is. 65:17-19)

During the coming reign of the Messiah, this restoration of the earth will be complete and perfect, but the Lord is giving us a taste of this joy now by watching Eretz Yisrael (the Land of Israel) blossom as the rose.

> "The wilderness and the wasteland shall be glad for them, and the desert shall rejoice and blossom as the rose; it shall blossom abundantly and rejoice, even with joy and singing." (Is. 35:1, 2)

One of my favorite things to do these days (surprisingly enough) is to hang the washing outside to dry on the sun-baked balcony. Situated high atop the mountain, I look out upon the landscape and drink in a partial view of what God sees when he looks upon the beauty of this land. I can picture King David looking out upon similar sunny balconies and red-tiled rooftops when he spied the lovely Batsheba. Middle-Eastern melodies, sung in Hebrew, are heard out many windows. The land is blossoming with joy and with singing.

Mountain of Death

Ariel, the largest Jewish settlement in the territory of Samaria, used to be known as *Har Heress,* (Hebrew for 'Mt. Destruction'), owing to its unusual barrenness. In local Arabic slang it was called 'Mountain of Death.' Arab village lore told of dreadful things that would befall those who dared to climb this mountain on which nothing would grow, and that even the Sheik's donkey could not be persuaded to climb it. When approached by Israeli representatives after the Six-Day War with an offer of purchase, the Arab leaders were glad to accommodate them – laughing in their sleeves, so the story goes, at the foolishness of the Jews to pay good money for such a cursed place where even goats could not graze. But, relying on Jewish ideals, security needs, and Biblical support rather than legend, the Israeli government signed a new settlement into life on the Mountain of Death. In 1978, the government authorized, on this bare height where even grass would not grow, the planting of the first 60 families. The rest, as they say, is history, but it has to be seen to be believed." [20] Scripture is fulfilled before our very eyes as the land is restored – why? It is because of the Lord's awesome and everlasting love for His people, Israel.

> **"I have loved you with an everlasting love; I have drawn you with loving-kindness. I will build you up again and you will be rebuilt, O virgin Israel. Again you will take up your tambourines and go out to dance with the joyful. Again you will plant your vineyards <u>upon the mountains of Samaria</u> and eat from your own gardens there and enjoy it undisturbed."** (Jer. 31:4, 5)

---

20 Gilboa, tova & Menachem and Gelbard, Tuvia, <u>Samaria Our Roots,</u> Feeling, Touching, Smelling the Bible, p. 66)

Partnership Between God And Man

Yes, this physical restoration of the land came about through human determination - through the blood, sweat and tears of Zionist pioneers - but what took root here cannot be accounted for by natural means alone. Even the Arabic peoples living in surrounding villages must admit that something supernatural has occurred.

> **"They will say, 'This land that was laid waste has become like the Garden of Eden; the cities that were lying in ruins, desolate and destroyed, are now fortified and inhabited.' Then the nations around you that remain will know that I יהוה have rebuilt what was destroyed and have replanted what was desolate. I, יהוה, have spoken, and I will do it."** (Ezek. 36:35, 36)

Since 1978, the tiny wilderness outpost of sixty families has grown into a thriving city of over 15,000 people. Not only did grass grow, but also lush gardens, parks, pine groves, vineyards – and a soccer field with turf that is the envy of many Israeli teams…[21]

It was the Lord who predicted the land would be made desolate, as part of the curse He pronounced upon Israel.

> **"They will turn my pleasant field into a desolate wasteland. It will be made a wasteland, parched and desolate before me; the whole land will be laid waste because there is no one who cares."** (Jer. 12:10, 11)

---

21 Gilboa, p. 67 (Tova & Menachem, co-owners of the Eshel Shomron Hotel in Ariel, were wounded in a terrorist attack in 2002)

Therefore, it is also God, in partnership with His people, who are restoring this land.

I heard once, of a story that I believe helps to illustrate this partnership. A man came across a deserted, neglected garden. All the flowers had withered and the vines overgrown the rocks. The earth was full of weeds and thistles. Each day for weeks, the man came to this patch of land and worked to restore the garden to its original beauty. He planted seeds, pulled the weeds, watered the flowers, and pruned the vines. Eventually, the garden was a wonder to behold and people came from all over the country to admire it. One day, a particularly religious man stood at the garden, raised his hands to heaven, and praised God for His marvelous works. The gardener replied, *"Yes, I praise God, the giver of the sun and the rain, and life itself, but you should have seen the mess this garden was in before I came along!"* This is not to belittle the wondrous works of the Lord, but only to remind us that we, too, have a part to play in God's plan upon this earth, and even in His plan to restore the nation of Israel. I am particularly touched by the bold, colorful, yellow and red tulips standing tall in proud testimony of the Christians Zionists who came from Holland to show their goodwill by planting their tulip bulbs on the mountains of Samaria.

Tulips planted by Christian Zionists in Ariel

Restoration of the Land

We, as people who belong to Him, cannot just sit back passively and expect Him to do it all. God sent the rain and provided the sunshine, but people worked hard to turn desert wasteland into a garden oasis. Some even gave their lives to drain the malaria-infested swamps. It was water that restored the land and it will be living water that will restore the people's hearts to their God. When God pours out His Spirit upon Israel, it will not be a drizzle, but a torrential downpour, such as we often experience in the winter in Israel. Still, people will need to labor hard in the harvest fields; some may even sacrifice their lives to help bring about the Spiritual restoration of Israel!

I try to take advantage of every opportunity to walk outside in this city amongst its stone buildings, just to gaze upon the abundance of flowers of every variety growing out of stone cliffs, and at the spectacular gardens. Each day, walking my son to 'gan' (kindergarten), we pass through a relatively undeveloped area of land. The tree branches hang to the ground, bowed over with bright yellow blossoms; others stand resplendent with violet orchids, and roses in full bloom – red, white, pink, yellow, peach, and various combinations. My son, who is more of the 'car and truck kind of guy' at this stage, sometimes loses patience with my oohs and aahs over the foliage. To him, when you've seen one flower, you've seen 'em all. But my exclamations of delight are not simply due to their physical beauty, but because of what they represent – the return of God's favor to Zion.(Psalm 102:13) The time of her punishment is over; now is the time the Lord is returning His blessings to Israel. The blooming of the land, which used to stand as a barren wasteland, testimony of God's wrath, now proudly proclaims God's delight in the land.

> **"You shall no longer be termed Forsaken, nor shall your land any more be termed Desolate (S'hmama); but your shall be**

called 'my delight is in her' (Hephzibah), and your land married (Be'ulah); for the Lord delights in you, and your land shall be married." (Isa.62:4)

Beautiful purple blossoms in the desert.

The restoration of the land foreshadow our betrothal to the Lord and the new life He will soon bring to the hearts of the people. Each flower in this land then, gives me hope and renews my faith in the promises of God. We need to see and recognize the signs of the times we are now living in. The only thing more tragic than missing the opportunity to partner with God in His restorative plan, is to miss the plan altogether due to ignorance of God's Word.

Tu Bishvat

On the festival of *Tu-Bishvat* (Festival of Trees), our family decided to take part in the planting of trees in the Jewish National Fund forest. As I knelt on the dry, rocky earth, cradling my own tiny sapling, I considered the miracle of the reforestation of this land and wept in gratitude to my merciful God. He does not treat us as our sins deserve; He does not stay angry forever, but always longs for reconciliation and restoration. My tears watered the little tree, realizing that this joyous time for the nation of Israel has come!

Planting trees for Tu Bishvat.

The following is a copy of an e-mail letter I sent out about this Festival of Trees with regards to the Restoration of Israel.

TU BISHVAT

Shalom from Jerusalem

Today (Feb. 8th, 2001), the 15th day of the Hebrew month of Shvat, is celebrated in Israel as:

Tu Bishvat - The Festival of Trees. This is not a Biblical holiday; the Torah contains no command to celebrate it, nor is it even mentioned. It is more of a national Israeli chag (festival). But it does have significance for us Bible believers, especially those who are interested in prophecy. Most are aware of the fact that for approximately two thousand years this land lay desolate, a wilderness, practically uninhabitable, void of vegetation. God warned His people over and over again, but they would not listen to the warnings of His prophets, and so He had no choice but to carry out all the curses of the Mosaic Covenant into which the nation of Israel willingly entered at Mt. Sinai. (Deut. 28)

The desolation of the land and exile of the people would stand as stark evidence of God's wrath to all the surrounding Gentile nations.

> "'The whole land is brimstone, salt, and burning; it is not sown, nor does it bear, nor does any grass grow there, like the overthrow of Sodom and Gomorrah, Admah, and Zeboiim, which the Lord overthrew in His anger and His wrath.' All nations would say, 'Why has the Lord done so to this land? What does the heat of this great anger mean?' Then people would say; 'Because they have forsaken the covenant of the Lord God of their fathers, which He made with them when He brought them out of the land of Egypt...Then the anger of the Lord was aroused against this land, to bring on it every curse that is written in this book. And the Lord uprooted them from their land in anger, in wrath; and in great indignation, and cast them into another land, as it is this day.'" (Deut. 29:23-28)

The prophet Jeremiah gave this reason as explanation for why God so devastated the physical land of Israel:

> "Why does the land perish and burn up like a wilderness, so that no one can pass through? And the Lord said, 'Because they have forsaken My Torah which I set before them, and have not obeyed My voice, nor walked according to it, but they have walked

> according to the dictates of their own hearts and after the Baals, which their fathers taught them.'" (Jer. 9:12-14)

This may also stand as a warning to us, that we must live in obedience to God's word, and not according to the dictates of our own hearts, nor even by family tradition - what our fathers taught us if it contradicts the Torah.

The good news is that our God is merciful and He promised a future time of restoration, when an ecological miracle would take place. The desert would blossom like a rose, the wilderness would be transformed into a Garden of Eden; trees would once again produce fruit; the land would be re-inhabited, the cities re-built. This time is now! It is God's appointed time to end the punishment and return his favor unto Zion, to choose Jerusalem and Israel once again.

> **"You will arise and have mercy on Zion; for the time to favor her, Yes, the set time, has come."** (Ps. 102:13)

> **"For the Lord will comfort Zion, He will comfort all her waste places; He will make her wilderness like Eden, and her desert like the garden of the Lord."** (Is. 51:3)

Where we lived in Jerusalem, contractors were building several apartment complexes across the street. The continual noise of the construction from early morning until night could potentially become a source of annoyance, but because of the word of prophecy, it was music to my ears. For the Lord is building Jerusalem. God's people are coming home. In preparation for the return of the exiles, God spoke to the prophet Ezekiel to prophecy to the mountains of Israel:

> "But you, O mountains of Israel, you shall shoot forth your branches and yield your fruit to My people Israel, for they are about to come." (Ezek. 36:8)

The custom in Israel on this day is to eat dried and fresh fruits from the trees and bless God, the creator of the fruit of trees. This reminds me of my early days as a child in Talmud Torah, an elementary Hebrew school in Canada. Each year on Tu Bishvat, we would each receive one dried carob pod to eat. These tasted (and smelled) terrible in our opinion, but we ate them joyfully simply because they came from the land of Israel. How ironic now, when I see those same dried carob pods, lying on streets and in the gutters like refuse.

Have you in the nations eaten any dried fruits from Israel? The prophet Isaiah knew by divine inspiration that one day Jacob would take root again in the land and then:

> "Israel shall blossom and bud, and fill the face of the world with fruit." (Is. 27:6)

Another custom practiced for both religious and secular Zionistic reasons is to plant a tree somewhere in Israel. This was something else we used to do in Hebrew school. Each year we would pay a token and receive a certificate that a tree had been planted in the Land of Israel in our name (or in honor of someone else's.) I remember our first year, riding the buses in search of a JNF (Jewish National Fund) forest to plant our sapling. After several transfers and missing our stop, we ran across the highway (what – no crosswalks?), chose our plant, dug and tenderly laid our little tree in the hole we had dug in the hard dirt with our hands. I wept as we realized our tiny contribution to the awesome fulfillment of prophecy for this land.

> "**And when you arrive in the land, plant all manner of fruit trees.**" (Lev. 19:23)

The Torah actually forbids people from destroying the trees during times of war.

> "**When you besiege a city for many days to wage war against it to seize it, do not destroy its trees.**" (Deut. 20:19)

Israel apparently is the only country in the world that is actually adding to their population of trees rather than reducing their numbers. We are reminded by this custom of planting trees that the restoration of the land of Israel is a miracle of God (Ezekiel 36), but it also has come about through partnership with man – through hard work and sacrifice, as well as irrigation.

I believe that the spiritual restoration of Israel, promised in the 37-th chapter of Ezekiel will happen in the same way. It will be a mighty move of God, the pouring out of the water of the Holy Spirit upon the land. But it will also require hard labor and sacrificial effort, like the first pioneers (Halutzim), who left home, country, and family for His name's sake. In the future in the New Jerusalem, fruit-bearing trees whose leaves will bring healing to the nations will line the sides of the river which flows from the sanctuary of God:

> "**Along the bank of the river, on this side and that, will grow all kinds of trees used for food; their leaves will not wither, and their fruit will not fail. They will bear fruit every month, because their water flows from the sanctuary. Their fruit will be for food, and their leaves for medicine.**" (Ezek. 47:12; Rev. 22:2b–3)

Land of Milk and Honey

It is not only with grass and flowers that the Lord is restoring the land; He is also blessing the crops of the land and the fruit of the trees and the bounty of the fields. Although some areas of the world experience famine, Israel need not fear famine in the future.

> **"I will increase the fruit of the trees and the crops of the field, so that you will no longer suffer disgrace among the nations because of famine."** (Ezek. 36:30)

Shopping at the open-air markets in Israel is truly an experience! It seems as if the one who hollers the loudest sells the most produce, therefore the hollering is tremendous. *Tohu v'vohu*, the Hebrew word for 'chaos' describes the scene on a Friday afternoon as last minute shoppers scramble for supplies before Shabbat, when the stores all close down. What is significant about these Israeli markets, however, is the incredible bounty of the produce. Fruits and vegetables here are full, ripe and taste wonderful.

Restoration of the Land

The word of God promises that,

> "The time will come when Israel will take root and bud and blossom and fill the whole earth with her fruit." (Is. 27:6)

This day has come in our generation, for Israel now exports her quality produce all over the face of the world.

> "For the Lord has given wonderful promises to Israel." (Num. 10:29)

Yes, the Lord also has wonderful promises for the Church, and she may claim some of these promises from the bible as the spiritual seed of Abraham, but many of these promises are specific to the physical nation of Israel.

> "You gave Israel this land that You promised their fathers long ago – a wonderful land that flows with milk and honey." (Jer. 32:22)

Israel is proving that the fulfillment of these prophecies is literal with regards to her, not simply spiritual, as some would like to believe. This land of Israel is not like any other nation of the earth, no matter how much people protest to the contrary and try to fit her into just another slot among the nations:

> "But the land you are crossing over to possess is a land of mountains and valleys that drinks water from the rain from heaven, a land for which יהוה your God cares; the eyes of יהוה your God are continually on it from the beginning of the year to the very end of the year." (Deut. 11:11-12)

Throughout the rainy season here, I think of this verse - that the land is drinking rain from heaven, and that the Lord has His eyes upon it continually.

Marvels and Wonders

Surely the Lord is fulfilling His promises to the young lad of twelve years old that He would show wonders to His people Israel and to the whole world.

> **"Therefore, behold, I will again do a marvelous work – among this people, a marvelous work and a wonder."** (Is. 29:14)

The Lord has already done a marvelous work in restoring the physical land of Israel itself, and bringing many of His children home. The final wonder, however, remains to be seen when the Lord returns to save Israel, to bring the rest of the Jews out of exile, and finally to restore His people to Himself forever. When this happens, surely the nations will be forced to admit that God has indeed done great things for Israel.

CHAPTER THREE

OUR PERSONAL EXODUS

When our family finally made the decision leave Canada, the land of our exile, to return to Zion, the land promised my Forefathers, we had nothing but God's word and the leading of the Holy Spirit. This was an incredibly huge leap of faith for us – to leave my beloved parents, family, friends, brothers and sisters in the Lord, many of whom pleaded with us not to leave them. After all, to drag our children half way across the world to an unfamiliar country without even knowing our specific destination? *'Must be meshuga'* (crazy), most people thought. Each year the Jewish community of my hometown would celebrate *Yom Haatzmaut* (Israel's Day of Independence) with great pride and fanfare. Israeli flags would wave in people's hands, and schoolchildren would sing Hebrew songs about the land of Israel. But to my husband and I, the festivities began to seem hollow, since no one in our comfortable Canadian community seemed to take the idea of returning to the 'Promised Land' seriously. But the Spirit of God would not allow this desire to return to Zion, a burning zeal, to be extinguished. The prophets said that even in these distant lands, we would remember our calling and would begin to yearn for Zion and Jerusalem.

"I will sow them among the peoples, and they shall remember Me in far countries;

> They shall live, together with their children,
> and they shall return." (Zech. 10:9)

Yes, we knew we were probably idealistic, and yes, we knew it would probably be more difficult than we had imagined, but we believed in God's word that this is a 'good land', not one that devours its inhabitants. We believed that if we went with the same confidence that Caleb and Joshua had in God's abilities, we would certainly survive to enter the land. And so, with nothing but a pile of debt from student loans and ministry expenses, we asked the Lord to provide. Within two weeks, our debt was completely and to the penny paid off through a generous gift from some of my students after their '*Mikvah*' (ritual water immersion - baptism).

We then heard of a 'seat sale' at the airlines – that we could purchase our tickets at a discount if we had the cash by the coming Monday (This was now Thursday). We asked the Lord, if it truly was His divine will and timing for us to return now, to provide for the tickets for all five of us. On Friday afternoon, two precious sisters from the ministry came by, giggling like young schoolchildren. With great joy and gladness, they handed me a check for the remaining amount of the tickets. Halleluyah! We now had tickets in hand, but absolutely nothing to live on once we reached the land until we could get settled. In a country where a simple breakfast plate can set you back 50 sheckels ($12 U.S.) and a family room in a hostel can cost $300 U.S., arriving destitute is not to be recommended. We carried on, however, teaching about Israel and the Jewish roots of Christianity in seminars and classes, trusting *Yehovah Yireh* (God who will see and provide). After one class, I was handed an envelope full of American one hundred-dollar bills! You can imagine the halleuyah shouts and dancing going on in our household. I repeat this account in order to give testimony of how God did a marvelous work and a wonder in leading us out of exile and back to the land of Israel. It also demonstrates that when we set our hearts and minds in a certain direction and rid ourselves of double mindedness about it, all heaven and earth will often move on our behalf to bring our desire to pass. We remain forever grateful to those who not only heard, but also acted upon the Word of God which exhorts Gentile believers to help the Jewish people return home, not only from Russia and Eastern Europe but from *all* the nations of the world.

> **"Behold, I will lift My hand in an oath to the Gentiles, and set up My standard for the nations; they shall bring your sons in their arms, and your daughters shall be carried on their shoulders."** (Is. 49:22)

Some of our brothers and sister would have dearly loved to actually carry our children back to the Land on their shoulders and in their arms if possible, but instead they provided the way. The Lord promises that as we give, so shall it be given back to us (Luke 6:38) and I believe that the Lord will mightily bless the precious people who gave materially towards our homecoming.

Heeding God's call to the land of Israel seemed a bit like jumping off a cliff. (I was never much for daring sports like skydiving). And yet, the unmistakable voice of the Lord told us to start packing by faith. God said to Jacob:

> **"I am with you and will watch over you wherever you go, and I will bring you back to this land. I will not leave you until I have done what I have promised you."** (Gen. 28:15)

We felt this a specific word of assurance and comfort. Within three months of the call, we left Canada – with great joy, but also many tears. A delegation of our family and friends came to the airport to see us off. Many were students who had been learning with us about the Jewish Roots of the Christian Faith. Most didn't feel ready yet to be on their own, left as if sheep without a shepherd.[22] We hadn't even covered the entire yearly cycle of the Feasts of the Lord yet; things happened so quickly. It sounds so easy when we skim through the Biblical account of Abraham leaving the security of home and land and family to venture into the realm of the unknown. But the reality of hugging my mother and father goodbye at the airport, not knowing when or if we would ever see each other again, was heart wrenching. At the last minute, my five-year-old son handed my mother his own

Leaving Canada.

---

22 Sadly, the group that carried on after we left eventually split with the majority of its members converting to Orthodox Judaism and leaving their faith in Yeshua.

little copy of the New Testament and asked her to read it for him while he is gone. She took it to her heart and promised that she surely would.

Yeshua also gave us this promise:

> "No one who has left home or brothers or sisters or mother or father or children or fields for me and the gospel will fail to receive a hundred times as much in this present age (homes, brothers, sisters, mothers, children and field – and with them, persecutions) and in the age to come, eternal life."
> (Mark 10:29)

Emanuel – God With Us

We stopped in Wales for three days, sharing with a group of believers at a wonderful 16th century farmhouse. As the taxi drove us from Wales to Heathrow airport in London, the sky grew dark and my youngest son fell asleep. We settled in for the ride, but I could not sleep, for I felt the presence of the Lord with us and a 'holy hush' filled the car. The scripture came to my mind, which had been repeated so often over the last few months that it became emblazoned forever upon my mind,

> 'Be strong and of good courage. Do not be afraid; do not be discouraged, for the Lord your God will be with you wherever you go."
> (Josh. 1:9)

Everywhere I looked, this verse stared back at me – in the Bible stories I would read my son, on a wall plaque, even as I sat to eat my food, this verse was glazed onto the ceramic plate! I think God was trying to make a point! A beautiful CD played 'Songs of Zion' and I wept as I listened to Maurice Sklar's[23] instrumental rendition of 'Go Down Moses – Tell Pharaoh, Let My people Go!" As we drove, I knew that one family of captives was returning home, and that the Lord was well pleased. As the tears streamed down my face, the sweet melody of the violin played from Fiddler on the Roof the Sabbath blessing, 'May the Lord protect and defend you; may He always keep you from harm; may you come to be a shining light in Israel....'" We gave Allen, the taxi driver, a hug and told him that this day, he had taken part in fulfilling prophecy:

> **"See, I will beckon to the Gentiles, I will lift up my banner to the peoples; they will bring your sons in their arms and carry your daughters on their shoulders."** (Is. 49:22)

Posing with Allen the taxi driver.

---

23   Songs of Zion CD by Maurice Sklar.

Bringing Back the Captives

British Airways aircraft was mercifully equipped with 24-hour cartoons for the children, but also with a scanner that showed exactly where the plane was flying. I eagerly watched on the screen as the plane flew over nations, closer and closer to Israel. I felt like a kid, bouncing on my seat, waiting impatiently for the biggest and best present of her life. Finally we landed and disembarked the plane. Stepping out onto Israeli soil, breathing the air, seeing the little orange trees, hearing the people speaking Hebrew, I beamed with joy! It was too good to be true. It was like a dream. We made it! We were home.

> "'When the Lord brought back the captives to Zion, we were like people who dreamed. Our mouths were filled with laughter, our tongues with songs of joy." Then it was said among the nations, 'The Lord has done great things for them. The Lord has done great things for us, and we are filled with joy.'"
> (Ps. 126:1-3)

Little did we know that the great things the Lord had done for us were only the beginning.

They Went Not Knowing Where They Were Going...

Once we arrived at the airport and gathered our huge hockey bags and enormous suitcases together, we then faced the decision – where do we go from here? This was the first, but not the last time we would ask this question. We had thought we could stay cheaply at Israeli youth hostels, but soon found out that this was myth number one. The

Timothy sitting on his suitcase with his monkey.

truth is that the only cheap thing in Israel is a McDonald's ice cream cone for two sheckels. Everything else seemed outrageously expensive. We had not yet learned where the 'locals' shop and where to find the bargains in the market (shook).[24] Obviously, with food and accommodation costs, we would very soon run out of money. Not seeing any alternative however, and exhausted from twenty four hours travelling without any sleep, we booked a room in a Tel Aviv hostel and set out to find a taxi. This in itself was a challenge - to find a taxi that would fit all five of us plus the

---

24   Open air Israeli market is called a shook in Hebrew

amount of luggage we towed along. The Israeli taxi driver (of a category that considers their passengers a lowly form of life) asked where we were going? We gave him the name of the youth hostel and he asked if we are Jewish. When I answered in the affirmative, he shook his head, declaring that surely we didn't want to spend our first Shabbat (Sabbath) in Tel Aviv; we most certainly wanted to be in Jerusalem. He promptly used his cell phone to cancel our reservation. And so we sat there. This was my first experience in finding out that in Israel, everyone is '*mishpachah*' (family), therefore our business is his business. We experienced many other examples of crossing boundaries that we Canadians feel comfortable with. At times the Israeli standard of acceptable boundaries could reach even into the most intimate details of life. One sales clerk, a complete stranger to me, even asked completely unashamedly if my husband is circumcised! ☺ We had a lot to learn about this new country. We entered as did Abraham, not knowing where we were going, and making our home in the Promised Land like strangers in a foreign country. (Heb. 11:89)

Meanwhile, the taxi driver impatiently asked where to take us. Spontaneously, I answered, '*Take us to Yad Hashmona*'. This is a Messianic Moshav (community) that I knew was hosting a Bead Chaim (Pro-Life Israel) conference that weekend near Jerusalem. I had corresponded with the director of Bead Chaim years previously, sharing my testimony about my son, Timothy, so it was my delight to spend my first Shabbat in the land together with the people involved in this ministry. The taxi dropped us off (along with all our luggage) in the lobby of Yad Hashmona but to our disappointment, we found that they were completely booked up for the weekend. I sat outside on the ancient yellow stones and cried and prayed and cried some more. My husband reassured me with God's promise that an angel would go ahead of us and lead us to the place prepared for us.

The director, hearing of our predicament, found us a place to lay our weary heads at a nearby hotel; the moshav graciously accommodated the luggage of these crazy Canadians in the lobby for the entire weekend; and I was asked to share my testimony the next morning at the conference.

Sharing my testimony at Yad Hashmona.

Divine Guidance

It was an honor and a privilege for me to testify to the assembly of Believers in the land about the goodness of the Lord – how he saved the life of my son from abortion and extended salvation to my children and I through Yeshua the Messiah.[25] Temporarily setting aside my concern for our immediate needs, I thrilled to hear the interpreter translate my testimony into Hebrew for the Israeli Hebrew speakers. We met Messianic believers and leaders at the conference that warmly welcomed us to the land. It felt like *mishpachah*

---

25 See book, Grafted In Again, or DVD Because He Lives, Hannah's personal testimony available by mail or through website:www.voice-forisrael.com

(family). After the morning session, a beautiful, English-speaking woman[26] approached us and asked if we had a place to stay. When I answered no, that we came by faith like Abraham, not knowing where to go, she made us an incredibly generous offer of her apartment in Netanya, a beautiful resort city, for an entire three months – free!. We couldn't believe the beautiful ocean view, and that just outside our door lay the sun, sand and sea of the Mediterranean coast.

Netanya beach.

"He who has compassion on them will guide them and lead them beside springs of water. I will turn all my mountains into roads, and my highways will be raised up. See, they will come from afar – some from the north, some from the west, some from the region of Aswan." (Is. 49:10-12)

And some, even from the frozen wasteland of Canada. Yes, the Lord has truly done great things for us.

---

26 This American woman, who had been a strong intercessor for Pro-Life Israel and helped many Believers in the Land began studying with Orthodox Jews and eventually fell away from faith, denying Yeshua and cutting off all contact with us and any other Messianic Believers.

The Battle for the Land

The challenge, of course, is to remember the wonder of the Exodus when the Egyptian army is hot on our tail! Most of those in authority in this land do not welcome the immigration of Jewish people who believe in Yeshua, and so it is a battle to claim our inheritance, but the battle is truly the Lord's. His faithfulness, goodness, and mercy endure forever. The law of return states that any Jewish person has the right to return to Israel along with their spouse and children and make this land their home. Unfortunately, however those in authority have ruled that anyone believing Yeshua is the Messiah may no longer be considered Jewish and therefore forfeits the right to Israeli citizenship. Believing, that our right to live as citizens in the land of Israel is not just a political decision but a divine promise, we hung on desperately even as our faith was being tested and stretched, seemingly beyond its limits. Joshua did not simply cross the Jordan and hand the tribes of Israel their inheritance on a silver platter; they had to fight and win many battles. In every victory God received the credit and the glory. So too does He receive the glory for our victory, since there is nothing we can do by ourselves in our own strength. The conquest of the land of Canaan seems to have happened quickly (we can read about it in one sitting), but it actually took seven years. For believers to not only enter, but to inherit their portion in the land is a battle today, not against flesh and blood, but against spiritual powers of wickedness. These forces of evil will do whatever they can to prevent believers from living amongst their Jewish brothers and sisters in the land. We have heard many testimonies of the trials of fire believers have endured in order to make this land their home. The Word of God, however, says

> **"We do not wage war as the world does. The weapons we fight with are not the weapons**

of the world. On the contrary, they have divine power to demolish strongholds. We demolish arguments and every pretension that sets itself up against the knowledge of God, and we take captive every thought to make it obedient to Messiah." (1 Cor. 10:35)

As I read and re-read the account of the conquest of the land, I could see that for each battle, God gave a specific plan and strategy to Joshua. And so we began to pray for a specific strategy for this battle. God, in His mercy, sent a beautiful Believer from the United States specifically to this mountain to intercede for Israel. Immediately after I had finished reading the portion about the battle of Ai (Joshua 8), the phone rang and this sister in the Lord began speaking about this exact same battle and then asked, *'How would you like to do something radical?'* At this point, I was ready to do almost anything, so I replied, *'Sure'*. She explained the strategy that God had given her. We were to take copies of our documents proving my Jewish heritage and that of my children and parents, and literally 'plant' them in the land. Halleluyah! We were declaring our right, by divine covenant through Abraham, Isaac, and Jacob, to be rooted and grounded in this land. We chose a plot of land belonging to a Christian Zionist and dug into a spot right next to a young fig tree. As we sang praises to God, we each planted our documents. Even the youngest child insisted on placing a copy of his own birth certificate into the dirt. We prayed and thanked God for His faithfulness to His own word that He would bring us back to this land and would settle us here. We then watered the ground, representing the watering of the Word by His Spirit; and we poured the water upon the fig tree, asking the Lord to pour out His Spirit, as He has promised, upon the House of Israel, represented by this young plant.

Planting our documents.

"And it shall come to pass afterward that I will pour out My Spirit on all flesh; your sons and your daughters shall prophesy, your old men shall dream dreams, your young men shall see visions. And also on My men servants and on My maidservants I will pour out my Spirit in those days." (Joel 2:28-29)

We asked the Lord to plant us, just as our names are planted, next to the fig tree (Israel), that we as Believers in Yeshua, might help bring nourishment to the roots and new life to the yet unbelieving nation. And so we stood by faith, **"Being sure of what we hope for and certain of what we do not see."** (Heb. 11:1)

Being homeless, however, was doing nothing for my emotional, physical, mental, and spiritual state. Also, I was pregnant again, feeling nauseous most of the time, and fretting about the possibility of another miscarriage and our lack of medical insurance. We found opportunity to house sit for a couple of families, but by the end of the week, it looked like we would be sitting out on the street. We kept hearing the horror stories, (almost like people who love to tell a pregnant woman about the horrendous birth experiences of their 'friends'), of believers who came to the land, tried to make Aliyah, even fought in the courts, and didn't make it. Just at the midnight hour though, the Lord miraculously came through for us.

I was reminded of several situations which occurred in Canada shortly before we left in which the Lord forewarned me that we would be in situations that seemed hopeless and impossible, but not to panic and not to give up. On the last day, a woman who had become a dear friend to us came rushing into the house, saying that she had noticed a little sign across the street about an apartment for rent. We immediately ran over to look at it. It was small, but clean and even had a stove! (Most Israeli apartments come completely unfurnished; that means no appliances and no closets.) The landlord was not so sure he wanted to rent to us vagabonds that he didn't know from Adam. *"Do either of you have a job?" "No." "Do you have your teudat zehut?"* (This is an identity card, which is required to do almost anything in Israel)

"No", I replied.

"So how can I be sure that you will pay your rent?", he demanded to know. How could we tell him that we had

faith God would provide? He said he could not rent to us just on the basis of a nice smile, and so he would consider us, but had others in mind. We went home and prayed. The next day, his wife suddenly and without notice walked into my friend's home, took my face in her hands and looked at me silently for a moment. In her eyes was love, but also something more.

"*Yes*", she said, "*I will tell my husband to rent to you and also to lower the price of the rent.*"

She then walked out, just as she came in, leaving us in a kind of stunned silence. We all spontaneously fell to our knees and worshipped the Lord. Signing a one year contract on the apartment that evening seemed like a significant step towards permanence, but we had yet to see it manifest in the natural.[27]

Our first landlords Tovah & Amitai with Timothy, Liat & me.

---

27 We heard news after we left Israel that Amitai had committed suicide, apparently an act of impulse after losing his job. Such was the economic pressure and despair upon some Israelis.

One day, my son came home from kindergarten carrying a fictitious *'teudat zehut'* with his photo on it. It was simply the children's activity for the day, but I received it as another sign from the Lord that the angels carrying these documents with them were already well on their way. It was only a matter of time and faith. We slept with this fake kindergarten document under our pillows every night.

Every so often, when one of us felt nudged by the Holy Spirit, we would visit our 'plot', water the documents, and pray for God's will to be done for us and for the young fig tree. But time was growing short. We had lived in Israel as 'tourists' for almost eight months, without income except what some generous soul sent to us. The last of our 'nest egg' had gone to pay the three months rent, which in Israel must be paid in advance. I was teaching English to several Russian and Israeli students privately in my home, which helped to meet our basic needs, but the issue arose over my eldest daughter's education. Without this identity number, it would be extremely difficult for her to continue her high school education in Israel, especially with the language handicap. Since the immigration to Israel from English speaking countries is merely a trickle at present, no provision is made for these students to receive assistance at school. Horror stories about the nature and condition of Israeli high schools abounded – of violence and chaos – confirmed by newspaper reports of stabbings and murders amongst Israeli youth. Although the Lord had established some tentative roots for her in this land, the yearning for the familiarity and security of life and family in Canada proved even more powerful. Feeling torn and undecided in this matter, we gave it over to the Lord together in prayer and asked Him to lead and guide her steps. The way opened wide for her return to Canada, and every doorway to find a way for her to remain in the land slammed shut in our faces.

Although the Lord seemed to be making His will for her at this time clear, I didn't think I could bear to lose her; to allow her to 'return to Egypt'. One day I happened to be left alone; I began to cry out to the Lord about my doubts and the pain in my heart to even think of letting her leave the land. The Lord took me directly to the account of Hannah. This story has special significance to me, as my name is Hannah and my son's is Shmuel (Samuel). When he was born, I also dedicated him to the Lord. But this time, the Lord spoke to me through this story about my daughter, showing me that just as the Hannah of the Bible had to release her son fully to God and trust Him with someone so precious, so must I release my daughter. I could not be a possessive mother, because our children all belong to the Lord first and foremost. He has His own plans and purposes for each one. And so we tearfully booked the one-way ticket for her to live with my family and finish high school in Canada. Although this was a heartache for us to be separated, God's grace prevented it from being more than we could bear. We trusted that God would use her as a light and a witness to our family in Canada, which He did. This move also opened the door for us to share with our family in Canada the reasons why we believe it is so important for us (and all Jewish people) to come home. In answer to their questions, I shared much prophecy with them. Halleuyah!

Because we needed to have my daughter's passport stamped, we went through the ordeal of storming the gates of the Ministry of Interior again. This is something that can barely be described, but must be experienced to be believed. The Lord had led us to transfer our file to the nearest Ministry office to Ariel, which happened to be the city of Petach Tikvah. But every time we called to inquire about the status of our file, we were told it had still not arrived from Netanya, or that it was at the moment still being scrutinized by someone in Jerusalem. Any further discussion or investigation proved fruitless, and so we had practically given up on ever trying to find our file, assuming that in the transfer, it had become lost somewhere in the desert on some donkey's pack sack!

But since we were forced to go for my daughter's sake, we lifted a sleepy little boy out of bed at 5:00 A.M., got everyone else up and dressed, and waited for the bus. Arriving at 6:00 A.M., we added our names to the list – we were already in a poor position of number 34. This could mean hours of waiting in a tiny, crowded, overheated office. We waited until 8:00 A.M. for the official to begin handing out numbers. As usual, the people argued and fought over whose number were whose. Thankfully, it was my husband who used his muscle to secure us our position. The last time, when he came alone, he told me that the battle was so fierce over these numbers that a physical fight nearly broke out between a religious woman and a Russian woman over who was first. Security actually had to be called. Yes, this is the 'Holy Land', but God surely has a work yet to do! Finally the doors opened and people began to storm the stairs. In another moment, I felt that I would suffocate, but the blockage of people suddenly burst and we made it into the Visa department office. My husband leaned over to me and whispered,

"*Don't even mention the issue of the passport. Ask first about our file.*"

Trusting his discernment, this is what I determined to do, but actually expected nothing. After waiting only a few minutes, a man walked by us and handed me something. It was his number – one of the first! Why he gave it to me, I don't know – I can only assume it was a miracle. It was our ticket into the bureaucrat's office.

"*Ken*" (yes), the official barked, not even looking up at us from the huge pile of papers layering her desk. She seemed annoyed that we were there, disturbing her 'work'. I said, in broken Hebrew, that we were there to inquire about our file. We all held our breath and she shuffled through piles and piles of papers and folders. I could hear my husband praying quietly behind me. I felt anxiety rising within me, but then some music on the intercom came through – '*Don't you Worry 'Bout a Thing'*. Can God actually speak through Stevie Wonder? Yet, I felt calmed decided just to sit back and keep my mouth shut and let God do what he wanted to do here.

"*No, nothing under that name.*"

"*Try my maiden name,*" I asked her. Shuffle, shuffle, sift, sort....

"*Wait – here it is – the last one in the pile,*" she said

Now came a kind of hurried reading through the official papers in our file. I could see all the copies of my documents proving my Jewishness, as well as all my protest letters to various government officials, with yellow highlighter marking several sentences. This woman called in another woman and they conferred together. You can tend to feel that they hold your very life's destiny in their hands, but we knew that God was in control here, and so we sat back and waited quietly.

Finally, before our very eyes, she began to process our application, saying that it was more than obvious that I am Jewish, and that we had waited long enough. She refused to question me any further about my faith. One hour later, an official handed me a small laminated card with my identity number and photo and said, 'Congratulations! You are now an Israeli citizen.' Halleluyah! A whole lot of shouts of joy and victory were resounding in our 'tent' that day! Our friends, who had stood with us in prayer and faith, wept with joy when they heard the news. We all knew that in the natural, what had just happened was impossible. But my briefcase, containing all our papers and documents also carries a card with five significant words on it, '*With God nothing is impossible.*' Only the week before, someone with an 'insider's connection', reported that the Ministry of

Interior stated we would receive citizenship '*over their dead bodies*'. People need to be awfully careful in boasting against the Lord. Preventing Jewish people from returning home to the land of Israel because of their faith in the Messiah, Yeshua, is definitely at odds with the will of God.

> **"It was not by their sword that they gained possession of the land, nor did their arm save them; it was your right hand, your arm, and the light of your face, for you favored them. You are my King and my God, who decrees victories for Jacob... In God we make our boast all day long, And we will praise your name forever."** (Ps. 44:38)

And just as God has been exceedingly good to us, so is *He determined to do good to Israel.*

> **"I am determined to do good to Jerusalem and to the house of Judah."** (Zech. 8:15)

CHAPTER FOUR

FACING THE GIANTS IN THE LAND

THE CHALLENGE OF KLITA (ABSORPTION)

Somehow, after this great victory, we expected our difficulties to have come to a end. Instead, we would soon discover that our greatest challenges were only beginning. The honeymoon phase was most definitely over. Somehow, we become so obsessed with Aliyah that we tend to forget about the process of absorption, called 'klita' in Hebrew.

The pressures of dealing with Israeli bureaucracy, traffic, politics, terrorism, schools, overcrowding, religious bigotry, rudeness, other elements of Israeli culture shock, had begun to take their toll. What could be described in Hebrew as a general state of 'balagan' (confusion, chaos, a real mess) in the country, was really starting to get to us. Not to mention our homesickness and cravings for 'real food' (oreos, doritos, and coke slurpies), the 'leeks and garlic' of Canada.' The Holy Spirit needed to rebuke us fairly regularly for moaning and complaining. We would, at times, stay up for hours just reminiscing about all the junk food we used to eat in

Canada. Really! After trying to navigate the bureaucratic jungle associated with klita (absorption), we came to the point of such disillusionment that we thought we would never encourage anyone else to make Aliyah.

One of the problems was that the new immigrants from the former Soviet Union, Eastern European countries, South America and other countries considered 'impoverished', or whose Jewish community suffers persecution, are given what's called a 'sal klita'. This is translated literally as an absorption basket. It includes healthy financial incentives in order to purchase appliances, furniture, and generally become minimally established with the basics to live in the Land. In teaching private English lessons, I came to know many Russian immigrants whose sole goal was to get out of Israel to America or some other country where it looked as if the grass was greener. And so, after sucking everything they could out of Israel's system, they would leave to greener pastures. One family of Russian Believers with ten children received a large amount of money when they arrived due to the size of their family. After one of the girls became pregnant out of wedlock however, and the other also began to get into trouble at school, they decided to return to Russia. They lied about their intentions, saying that they were only going back for a visit, in order that they would not have to pay back the money they had received from the Israeli government. This happens all too often. We, so-called 'rich Canadians', on the other hand, were given practically nothing. Our landlords, God bless them, provided us with dishes, pots and pans, a bed, some furniture, and a welcoming smile. Other friends pitched in to help us get a second hand fridge.

One thing we lacked, however, which seemed a real hardship to us was a washing machine. The settlement where we lived operated no coin laundry. I was pregnant again and experiencing fatigue and morning sickness. Washing a family of four's clothing by hand day after day (in the shower yet...) was something I was quickly growing tired of. My good friend and neighbor, bless her heart, allowed us the use of her washer, but it was tough to haul heavy baskets of wet laundry every day up and down several flights of stairs. Every government office we visited said there was nothing they could do for us since we had immigrated from a 'rich country'. There was simply no help available.

Christians for Israel

At the same time, a Christian group from the United States came to the settlement to perform Hebrew songs, to encourage the people in their weariness over life in Israel, and to hand over a $30,000 cheque to the mayor's representative. You would think that out of this huge sum, we could squeeze a measly second hand washer, but no... At one point, (just before the baby's birth), we had piles and piles of big garbage bags full of laundry sitting in our apartment. (My friend's machine also went on the blink). We knew we were supposed to thank the Lord in all things, and so instead of our usual complaining, we began to thank the Lord. We went all through the apartment, thanking the Lord for the piles and piles of dirty, stinking laundry, laughing at the outrageousness of such a statement. Right after this sacrifice of praise, however, the Lord came through with a washing machine for us. Just in time. He is never late! The whole incident even gave us opportunity to share about the Lord with the washing machine repairman. But for a time, I thought that our absorption process would fail and that we would end up back in Canada saying that the whole thing was brought down by a washing machine! Such is the reality of making Aliyah from the 'West'. It takes incredible determination and perseverance. Perhaps one day, when more North Americans immigrate, such injustices may decrease, but for now, they continue.[28]

It grieves the hearts of some of the Israeli Messianic Jewish Believers, many of whom are struggling to survive in the Land, to see Christian ministries and individuals donating substantial sums of money to the secular government of Israel or to Orthodox Jewish organizations or Yeshivas (schools of learning) rather than the Body of Faith in the Land. This is a little like someone feeding and clothing the poor and needy of their city, but leaving their own children to run around hungry and in rags. Often these Orthodox Jewish organizations and schools, funded by Christians, turn around and persecute Jewish Believers – burning down Bible bookstores, Messianic congregations, and Believers' homes. As Jewish Believers in Yeshua, we are mishpachah (family) with our Christian brothers and sisters in the Lord. Those who don't provide for their own families first and foremost are said according to the Bible to be worse than infidels. Paul's exhortation to the Gentile Church to repay with material blessings their debt owed to the Jews for the spiritual blessings they have received through them is usually misapplied to 'Jews' in general. In reading the context of this scripture (Romans 15:25-27), Paul's intention is clearly to take up a collection for the poor among the Jewish SAINTS (Believers in Yeshua) of Jerusalem. I hope that Christians with a heart for Israel will draw upon our experience as Believers in the Land to use discretion in their giving of material blessings to Israel and give first priority to the Messianic Jewish Believers and ministries in the Land.

It is one thing to bring Russian Jews back to the Land, but

---

28 As of December 1st, 2002, this inequality has been rectified by a new law giving financial incentives and benefits (called a sal klita or absorption basket) equally to new immigrants from any country, including North America and Western Europe. We wish this was retroactive!

quite another to put down roots and survive here. This also often requires financial support until the fragile tendrils have gained strength to remain in the ground. To simply dump plane loads and boat loads of immigrants into an already overloaded Israeli social assistance network is to invite more and more problems into the country: homelessness, prostitution, illegal drug trade, organized crime, alcoholism, and domestic abuse. This is only adding another burden upon a country that is already seemingly ready to cave in. The best way to reach the Jewish people is with an indigenous, local body of Jewish Believers in Yeshua. The best way to build up the body of Messiah in Israel is to send financial support directly to the local Messianic congregations and ministries who can help the Believers in tangible ways. What good is our faith, James exhorts us, if a brother or sister is without clothes or daily food and we say, "Go, I wish you well, I'll pray for you brother..." but do nothing about their physical needs? This kind of faith without its expression in our material giving is dead. (James 2:14-17) The scriptures exhort us to be open handed towards the poor in the land and God will bless all the works of our hands. (Deut.15:7-11)

Putting Down Roots

The first thing we needed to do in Ariel, was to establish a source of income and get the children in school. We registered my son in the Daati (religious) gan (Hebrew kindergarten), since we had heard that discipline and care is a bit better there than in the secular system. We were glad to have followed this advice, as he was happy and well taken care of there and the teachers were very kind women to this little boy of mine from Canada. The first day after registering him there, I was speaking English to someone and suddenly heard a shriek! It was a mother of one of the children who heard English being spoken and was so excited to meet another English speaking mother. Shelly had made Aliyah from South Africa and we became good friends, having our babies at the same time, and often walking them down to the town square to meet for coffee and a visit.

Shelly, Hannah & the boys on Yom Ha'atzma'ut (Israeli Independence Day)

Later, we found out that her mother, Ruth, was a Believer living in England, but Shelly had not spoken to her mother for twelve years over the issue of her mother's faith in 'Jesus'. Shelly, like most traditional Jews, perceived her mother as having betrayed God, the Jewish people and her Jewish heritage. We had many opportunities to share with Shelly about Yeshua from a Jewish perspective. She even began to attend our women's bible study and prayer meeting with us. Shelly finally reconciled with her mother and even invited her to visit in Ariel where we had a chance to meet and pray together. Ruth thanked God that He had led us to this settlement of Ariel to befriend her daughter and share with her the love of Yeshua. We need to trust the Lord that He will place us just exactly where he wants us, even where a lost lamb lives who needs to meet the Good Shepherd.[29]

Another woman that God brought into my life in Ariel was named Dahlia, a single mother with a little boy named Asaf. Dahlia's family had immigrated years prior, when she was just a little girl, from the nation of India. Through unfortunate circumstances, Dahlia ended up divorced and raising her little boy on her own – an exceedingly difficult task especially in Israel, where the kind of support systems for single parents we are used to in Western countries just don't exist in Israel. I used to see her, sitting on her steps, just staring out at the distance; she seemed terribly lonely and depressed. The Lord put on my heart to ask her if she wanted to learn English. This she was happy to do, so she used to come over each week for an English lesson. Eventually, we became friends and she was able to confide in me about her loneliness and despair over her life. One morning, I woke up with a picture of Dahlia's face in my mind; she was crying. Because it was Shabbat morning, I knew she would likely be home, so I phoned and asked if I could come over. She agreed immediately and was happy to see me. I knew that this was the opportunity the Lord was giving me to share my faith with her and the hope we have in Yeshua. Using her own Hebrew Bible, I shared about the Messiah and my own personal testimony. She wanted to receive Him too and prayed with me in Hebrew; it was as very precious moment. Through her tears, she said that when she woke up that morning, she heard a voice clearly say, "Talk to Hannah. She can help you." Halleluyah! When we moved away from Ariel, one of the most difficult things for me was to leave Dahlia. This is when we have to trust in our heavenly Father to keep those we commit to Him.

---

29 Shelly eventually separated from her husband, who was an Iraqui born Jew, charging him with assault. As a single mother trying to raise three little boys, life in Israel became exceedingly difficult. Shelly was afraid to profess faith in Yeshua in case her ex-husband used the information in the courts to take her children away from her. Eventually we lost contact with one another. Ruth eventually felt called to make aliyah as well but the attempt failed and she returned to England terribly disillusioned with Israel and especially with the Body of Believers in the Land.

Dahlia, Asaf, Liat and Timothy.

As Jewish Believers living in the Land of Israel, our hearts continually cried out for the salvation of our people. But God also gave us opportunities to share the gospel with Arabs as well. On our first visit to the Old City of Jerusalem, we stopped into a little restaurant that served pizza slices on the back of pieces of cut up cardboard cereal boxes. It was at Cardo Café in the center of the Jewish Quarter that we first discovered Sachlab. What? You don't know sachlab?! You haven't truly lived until you have tasted this delicious Middle Eastern hot, sweet, cinamonny flavored drink, served only in the winter. Its consistency is like thin, cream of wheat porridge and it sure warms the body and soul after a day of walking through the Old City in the middle of Israel's damp winter weather. It was also here at the Cardo that we first met Abed. Serving pizza straight from the large ovens, Abed's friendly, talkative manner immediately put one at ease. Perhaps he had a bit of a crush on my teenage daughter, but Abed delighted in explaining to us the whole pizza making and baking process.

Courtney & Abed at the Cardo Café

We came to know Abed as a good-hearted, extremely likeable young man who loved everyone regardless of race or religion; the kind of guy who would give someone the very shirt off his back. We were more than a little surprised to find out that Abed was an Arab, working in a Jewish café in the Jewish section of the Old City of Jerusalem. When we asked him about his religion, Abed admitted to being a 'nominal Muslim', but said that he knew about Jesus. We got to know Abed better over the years and became good friends; he came to all our children's birthday parties and often joined us in our home for Kabbalat Shabbat, the festive meal and ceremony on Friday evening to welcome the weekly Sabbath.

He even did his best to help find us an apartment when we were lost and homeless. On several occasions, we had opportunity to share the Lord with Abed; and one time my husband stayed up almost all night with him, sharing the gospel message of salvation with him. In the end, Radek asked Abed if he would like to receive Yeshua as his Lord and Savior. Abed declined, saying he was not ready. My

Facing the Giants in the Land

Abed with Timothy & Liat at our apartment.

husband warned him, based on his own personal life experience, that when we refuse the Lord, He has ways of drawing us near. What we didn't know then was that this would be a chilling prophecy in Abed's life.

The next day, we received a call. It was Abed, calling from the Jerusalem Police Station. Something had happened, he said. It was very serious. Abed was in deep trouble – he had killed an Israeli army officer. We were absolutely shocked! As the story unfolded, according to Abed, this officer was a known homosexual who aggressively came after Abed with perverted sexual advances. Abed claimed to have simply struck out in self defense and not to have known until he was arrested that the man was dead. It was in the middle of the Palestinian Intifada that this happened; Abed seemed to fall through the cracks of the Israeli justice system. He was sentenced to life in prison and is still serving his sentence now. Radek went to visit him in prison and brought him an Arabic Bible. "Do you want to receive Yeshua now?" Radek asked. "Yes, I do." Was Abed's humble reply.

Radek with Abed and his family in prison.

Abed was faithful to call us each and every week from prison, but it was not easy to visit him. He was often beaten and several times went on hunger strikes to obtain better treatment. At one point, he began to dictate to me his life story, but it sits incomplete somewhere in a file. I still write to Abed, by faith, as he cannot write me back. I tell him he is not forgotten. I write to him about Joseph in the Bible who also spent years in prison, and about the mysteries of God's ways with mankind. Occasionally he sends a message to us through some friends that he is still alive. He never complains; always says he is well. Out of all his many friends and, except for his immediate family of mother and sister (his father passed away), we were the only ones he trusted enough to call. After we left Israel for a season, I heard of a man with a prison ministry in the Land so I contacted him, pleading with him to visit Abed. Weeks later, his reply arrived, saying that Abed is a convicted terrorist and he refuses to visit him. Probably only God knows what truly happened between Abed and that Israeli army officer that day; but this one thing I know – I miss Abed, my friend.

It took awhile to get used to this aspect of life in Israel – the continual threat of violence, the constant presence of soldiers on the streets with huge guns strapped over their shoulders. One day, Timothy shouted out on the bus and pointed, "Look Mom! There's a soldier! And Mom – he's wearing a kippah!![30]" Everyone on the bus laughed. And yet that is the miracle and in a sense the beauty of Israel – that we know have our own army, the IDF, young men and women who stand ready to defend our nation with their lives. Never again will we be led like lambs to the slaughter, to be herded into cattle cars and shoved into Nazi gas chambers and ovens to be burned like pieces of garbage. No, we have an army now, backed by the Lord of Hosts, YHVH T'zva'ot, Captain of the army. And in the natural, Israel is totally outnumbered, but greater are they who are with us than those against us in heavenly realms. If God be for us, who can be against us? The barbed wire surrounding the settlements, the heavy wire mesh over the windshields of certain buses, the relentless security and searches at the entrance of every single office and store, did not inspire fear, but a sense of gratitude to God for this nation where we may take refuge.

Timothy posing with Israeli soldiers.

---

30 A kippah is a round headcovering worn by religious Jewish men indicating their respect for God

My husband, although denied citizenship, was given a work visa and obtained a position immediately with a ministry in the land. It was a real blessing to have a paycheck coming in, but it was also tough. I was pregnant and not feeling well. Pregnancy at the age of forty-two is just not the same as the same condition at the age of twenty. We never did find out what was wrong, but from about the sixth month on, I could barely walk or move around without a great deal of pain. My husband worked the night shift for this ministry, and had to travel by bus to Tel Aviv from the settlement. The bus ride took two hours there and two hours back. This was four hours a day extra travelling time, besides the fact that he usually worked overtime, and so was gone and average of 14-16 hours a day. On top of this, he was attending ulpan (intensive Hebrew classes) at night school, three hours at night and studying to pass the course. As if this wasn't enough, he also chose to take his driver's license at the same time, which meant a lot of lessons and practice time. For a long while, the only time I saw him was when he sat at the table to wolf down some food with bleary eyes, and stagger out the door. Poor him... poor me!! You can imagine that this situation was soon to become intolerable. We somehow survived – but the neglect of our new marriage and blended family during this vulnerable time of my life took its toll. Since I had already been abandoned in pregnancy once before this present marriage, this brought up for me the same feelings of fear, anger and resentment. Since we moved to Israel only a few months after our marriage, the stresses, changes and traumas of life prevented us from laying a solid foundation for our new life together as a couple and a family. It was not only our loads and loads of physical baggage that we brought with us to Israel, but also heavy spiritual and emotional baggage from each of our past that we dragged with us to this new land. Neither of us knew how to deal with it and so we chose to ignore and avoid all the red flags and warning signs.

God, however, is merciful and does not give us more than can bear; and so, by His grace, Courtney at this time returned to Israel to help me just before and after the birth of Liat. After being enrolled in school back in Canada for only about a month, Courtney called with some shocking news. My brother and his wife had suddenly separated. We knew that all was not well in their marriage, but didn't realize it had come to this point. Obviously, Courtney could not live alone there with my brother, and so she had nowhere else to live. She asked, "Mommy, can I come back home to live with you in Israel?" Music to this mama's ears, I can tell you that! We have a picture of Courtney with dirty rags, scrubbing the oven, with a caption underneath in our scrapbook that reads, "Cinderella".

Courtney as Cinderella

Courtney was indeed, like a Cinderella for the last month of my pregnancy, taking over the household, since I was confined to bed rest. What a blessing. It was hard for her to say goodbye to everyone she loves so much all over again, but we both agreed that it was the sovereign hand of God in her life, which brought her back to the Land. This time she did not come because of her Mom or her family, but of her own free will, not knowing that the time that God had a most wonderful blessing in store for her through her obedience and courage – a Godly husband! Although the Ministry of Interior held out for over two years, we now held in our hands citizenship cards for myself and our children. This was a great victory. We needed only to be still and know that He is God. It was not by our hand that we gained possession of our place in the Land but by His sword and the power of His right arm! (Ps. 44:3-8) My husband had yet to obtain his citizenship but we did not expect any real difficulties, since the law states that as the spouse of a Jewish Israeli citizen, he should also automatically be granted citizenship as well. Only now do we realize how naïve we really were at the time. Israel's Ministry of Interior is a law unto itself. They have absolute power and do not need to give any explanation or defense for their decisions. When they decided to take away even his temporary visa and refused to give him a work visa, all of my husband's pleas for the right to work in the country to feed his wife and children fell on deaf ears. "Go back to where you came from.", they replied. But we did not know this at the time. We still thought that it was just a matter of time before my husband, also would obtain citizenship. Because he was born in Poland and documents were either lost or hidden during and after the war, the issue of his lineage remained unclear. And so we carried on in faith.

A Better Place Prepared for Us

One of the things that greatly encouraged me during my pregnancy was meeting a delightful sister in the Lord named Hallel (meaning praise in Hebrew, as in hallel-u-yah) who lived in a neighboring settlement. She had announced during a Shabbat service at the local messianic congregation that the Lord had directed her to sell all she had and give it away to the poor. She said that the Lord told her "He was preparing a better place for her." Since her children had all grown up and left home, she was planning to move to a new, smaller apartment – this 'better place' that He had prepared for her in advance. Anyone who was in need could come to her home and pick up their hearts' desire. As we were short on furniture as well as sheckels, we went to visit Hallel and were so touched by the love of God that flowed through her being. She was full of joy in a way I have rarely seen before. Since she had a daughter a couple of years older than my teenage daughter, Courtney, I shared with her my concerns about her schooling. Hallel, as well as her daughter, gave me hope that if they could do it, so could we. Her daughter opted for the home schooling route, even though her Hebrew was fluent, because she couldn't cope with the cultural differences and the heavy spiritual darkness that operates in the Israeli schools. Hallel prayed for us with great enthusiasm and I felt refreshed and renewed. Her daughter even gave Courtney a few special posters and articles from her own room and wrote a personal note of encouragement to Courtney with her phone number on it. Thank you God for young women like that!

We picked out a few things we thought we could use – a sofa bed, a rug, a lamp, some kitchen things. And then Hallel, seeing the advanced stage of my pregnancy and my difficulty in walking, suggested we take the living room suite which included a beautiful, comfy, rocking chair/recliner. *"Oh- this would be too much"*, I thought. But she insisted. She also gave us a beautiful set of pottery dishes as well as a china set for shabbat. I was really overwhelmed and came home feeling so loved by both Hallel and by the Lord. I offer this testimony to you as a real example of how the Lord can and will provide all of our needs according to His riches in Messiah Yeshua. But the story of Hallel also testifies of another, deeper spiritual message.

What we didn't know then, was that the Lord was not speaking to Hallel about an earthly apartment, but a heavenly one. Approximately one month after our meeting, Hallel went to visit her daughter, who was eight months pregnant, in Ireland. In one fateful second, a vehicle hit their car in a head on collision and Hallel, her daughter, and the unborn baby were instantly killed. Yeshua answered, when a man asked Him what else we must do to inherit eternal life (besides keep the Ten Commandments) –

> **"If you want to be perfect, go, sell your possessions and give to the poor, and you will have treasure in heaven."** (Matt. 19:17-21)

Hallel may not have been perfect in herself, but she is certainly perfect in Yeshua's sight and we know that she is now in a better place that He has prepared for her, enjoying the treasure that she laid up in heaven while living here on earth. As I later spent many hours rocking my baby to sleep in Hallel's rocking chair, I often meditated upon this truth.

Childbirth in Israel

Pre-natal care in Israel is definitely unique and giving birth quite the experience in Israeli hospitals. Accustomed to the Canadian standards of health care, I was amused to discover that for a blood sugar test, I had to bring my own cup and lemon from home. Having had a home birth for my last baby, I wished to do the same for this one. But I found that Israel is not as accepting of home births and midwives as North America, and to receive her birth documents, should I decide to give birth at home, would be a bureaucratic nightmare. After tangling with the Israeli bureaucracy for so many months, this was not a prospect that we looked forward to. And so, after much prayer and seeking direction from the Lord, I consented to an Israeli hospital birth. Thus began the search to find a hospital that would allow a more natural child birthing experience and twenty-four hour rooming-in for mother and new baby. This proved difficult, but we persevered. We found a hospital in Kfar Sava which had one natural birthing room with a Jacuzzi and we prayed that this room would be available. Thankfully, since most women in Israel opt for an epidural anesthetic to numb the pain of labor and birth, the room was indeed divinely reserved for us. The Jacuzzi was a special blessing for me and a private message to me from my God who knows the secret desires of our hearts. For the past year, we had no bath, just a shower stall in our apartment in Ariel. God knew that I longed for a nice, hot soak in a tub. Well, because of the intensity of the labor, it was not really the relaxing Jacuzzi soak that I had envisioned, but still it was better than nothing!

Israel seems to have a standard maternity hospital policy that takes newborn infants into the nursery at night 'so that the mothers can get a good night's sleep'. This, however, ran contrary to my passionate beliefs about the necessity of mother-baby bonding and I was horrified to think that they would rip my newborn away from me to cry alone in a hospital nursery all night. We prayed about this and the Lord in this too, guided and helped us. I spoke to the head of the infant nursery and found out that it would be possible to sign a legal form, releasing the hospital staff from responsibility for my baby at night and keeping her with me in my room.

This settled, we waited for the great event. Since the timing of labor and birth can be unpredictable, we faced the probability of having to move quickly once things got underway. My husband would have to get home from Tel Aviv, even in the middle of the night when buses don't run, and we would have to drive over an hour to the hospital from the settlement. Thankfully, my husband's supervisor came to our rescue by driving him home and driving us both to the hospital when the labor pains became frequent and intense. I suppose they became a little too frequent and intense for this poor driver and he panicked. I couldn't help but laugh out loud at his erratic driving, as he raced down the side road, swerving around Arabs riding on their pokey donkeys, honking continually on his horn and screaming in Hebrew with his head out the window to the other drivers,

"Move over! Get out of my way! She's going to give birth in my van!!"

Only in Israel...

The labor was so intense that I was reminded of the scripture, **"Unless he cut short the time, none would survive."** (Matt.24:22) It seemed to me that even through this birth, the Lord was speaking prophetically. The medical personnel began to warn that things were not progressing and that I would not be able to have the natural birth experience I wanted. But the women's prayer group went to war for us again, and praise God, that baby was born in that Jacuzzi and T.V. room very shortly after the nurses' pronouncement of trouble.

On November 25th, 1999, I gave birth to our first 'Sabra' (native Israeli) – a little girl we named Liat.

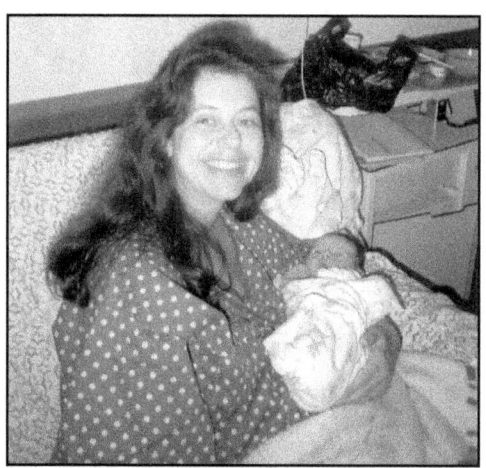

We chose her name from Isaiah 43:1:
"I have called you by name, you are mine[31] **(Li-atah)."**

---

31 See article, You are Mine, in articles archives on website:www.voiceforisrael.com

Liat

  This is the masculine form; we changed it to the feminine Li-at. We gave her the middle name of Stephanie after my husband's mother who passed away in Poland just after we married in Feb. 1998. Despite the fact that I signed the papers granting me twenty four hour rooming in, the nursing staff continued to beg and plead with me to let them keep the baby in the nursery at night. The first night, I finally allowed them to take her to the nursery with the other babies just on a trial basis. They assured me that if she even let out a little peep, they would bring her straight to mama. They even wrote in Hebrew on a piece of paper towel the instruction, "If this baby cries, bring it to mother in room_____" They draped this note across her little chest. Half an hour later, I peeked into the nursery. There was Liat, screaming her little head off, face red as a beet, with no one paying the least bit of attention – sign still across her chest! That was it – she stayed with me for the rest of my hospital stay. God has such a sense of humor and timing. He placed an Ethiopian woman in the bed next to me who had also just given birth to her fourth child. When the nurse came to take her baby to the nursery at night, she became incensed:

"I've had four children and no one is taking my baby away from its mother right after its born!", she declared. The nurses also became angry and a huge argument ensued, as is typical in this strife-filled country.

"Psst!", I called from behind my cloth partition.

"I know of a way you can keep your baby." And I explained to her the legal loophole. She was very grateful and we went together, like co-conspirators, to kidnap our babies out of the nursery and bring them to our room for the night. God is so good. He cares so much about mothers and babies.

> **"He tends his flock like a shepherd; He gathers the lambs in his arms and carries them close to his heart; he gently leads those that have young."** (Is. 40:11)

When it came time to take Liat home, my husband was incensed to find out that the hospital clerk would not put his name on the baby's documents as her father. Why? Because he didn't have a teudat zehut (identity number). He was still at this point, living on a tourist visa because if they can make anything difficult for you they will.[32] This I have come to

---

32 Withholding of documents such as passports and identity cards is a favorite tactic of the Ministry of Interior to persecute Messianic Believers and drive them out of the Land. At this time we continue to wait over a year for renewal of Radek's temporary visa, without which he cannot work, travel, or even have our children listed on his identity card.

believe, is the bureaucracy's prime reason for existence. Their attitude, (I would have to agree with my native Israeli brother in law), is *"if not for you, I could be having a coffee break!"* We did finally get this matter sorted out, Praise the Lord, and our sweet Liat, does now in fact, carry the name of her father. But all these kinds of humiliating encounters inflicted wounds in an already damaged sense of self, causing Radek to feel even more like a 'second class citizen', unworthy, and somehow inferior to others. He had already experienced these emotions as a new immigrant in Canada and going through it again re-opened those old wounds that had never truly healed. Resentment built up and began to fester into expressions of anger and hostility towards the Israeli government and people.

We were so proud, however, to show off Liat's Hebrew birth certificate and Israeli passport with her little baby's face on it. We wanted to send out birth announcements with her photo and a caption underneath saying, "**This one was born in Zion**." I felt that I had personally played a part in fulfilling prophecy – that we would not only return to the Land, but would multiply and bear young on the mountains of Israel. (Ezek. 36:11) One evening, while walking along the main pedestrian mall in Jerusalem, Ben Yehudah, a shop owner took notice of the baby, by then eighteen months old, toddling along beside us. *"How adorable she is!"*, he exclaimed. *"Where is she from?"* He asked. It was with great pride that we could answer, *"From Israel!"* God has a special register for the specific purpose of recording the ones who are born in Zion.

> **"The Lord will write in the register of the peoples; This one was born in Zion."**
> (Ps. 87:6)

The Educational Giant

After Mom and baby were settled in at home, we turned to the issue of Courtney's education. This turned out to be a real problem. My daughter, Courtney, is a trooper; she is not one who gives up easily, nor someone afraid of hard work. She is neither shy, nor aloof; she makes friends very easily in new situations. But this poor girl came home from a couple hours at the local high school in tears every day. She told horror stories of gangs, and screaming teachers all day long; of students getting locked in classrooms and busting doors down with their feet; that no one knew she was there or cared to know; that she didn't understand one word of Hebrew in the classroom and that no one would help her. She didn't even know where to go or if she was in the right classroom. If she asked anyone, they would only scream at her in Hebrew. This is an extremely unfortunate aspect of life in Israel – the deplorable state of the Israeli public school system. For English speakers who come at this age without Hebrew it is very, very tough to integrate. Some choose to home school.[33] That may be a good option for some, but for families who come here not to visit but to stay, learning the language fluently necessitates being in a Hebrew-speaking environment. The problem is that the Israeli powers that be changed the laws so that now new immigrants must compete

---

33 Home schooling has very recently (2002) become a technically legal option in Israel, but only with permission of the Ministry of Education. This required months of bureaucratic maneuvers, psychological testing and intrusive visits from social workers which, in the end, usually prove fruitless. Most Israeli homeschoolers educate their children at home under cover, not openly. There are presently two Messianic Elementary schools in the country – one in Jerusalem and one in Tiberius. Home schooling is generally not accepted in Israel as the norm is to put children in communal care type situations at an early age – usually by six months – as both parents usually need to work for economic reasons and the 'it takes a village to raise a child' philosophy is prevalent in Israel.

in their high school exams with native Israelis in the Hebrew language. This is impossible. We searched for alternatives and didn't find any in Jerusalem. One of the challenges is the lack of availability of consistent and accurate information. Most likely, by the time you find out the information you need, the rule will have changed, or alternatively, the person you talked with did not know what they were talking about and the next person you speak with will tell you the opposite. Such is life in Israel!

The only solution we could see was to send Courtney to a boarding school again in a city about an hour away and to have her come home on Shabbat and holidays. It was not what either of us wanted. Courtney was like a second mother to Liat. She had rocked and held her each day and night for a month. When we left her there at the boarding school, I had to take Liat out of her arms, and we both sobbed. It felt like ripping a child away from its mother. But we seemed to have no other choice. Courtney still struggled in this program and seemed on the point of a breakdown. I told her to pack her bags. We knew of a Christian English speaking school for children of diplomats and international students in Jerusalem. Even though the tuition cost over $10,000 per year, I refused to sacrifice my daughter's health and sanity. I also would not allow the enemy to pluck us up out of this Land over this issue. Once the boarding school saw that she was leaving for good and that we were very serious about this, the principal called Courtney into his office and admitted that they have a special program for new olim (immigrants) which teaches in Hebrew but at an easier level and gives special assistance to the students. Now he tells us! This is the way it is in Israel; one must show a fierce determination before anyone will take you seriously. The class was designed for Russian and East Europeans immigrants, but they finally allowed in our Canadian daughter. God makes a way where there is no way.

Courtney[34] graduated from high school at the top of her class with a 95% average, which is unbelievable, but she worked very, very hard. Students must read entire chemistry and biology textbooks in Hebrew. I don't want to discourage anyone from coming if they have teenagers, but just to be prepared, so that arrangements can be made for long distance education before leaving, or by simply knowing that in Israel, this is one of the giants we must face and with God's help, find a solution.

---

34 In March 2002, Courtney married Emanuel, a Messianic Jewish young man from Jerusalem. He is a gifted praise and worship leader, composer and musician; he also happens to be the pastor's son (If the rabbi has only one son, why not? ☺) Their love story and wedding has been a powerful 'true love waits' testimony to many young people and singles. DVD available by mail or through website: www.voiceforisrael.com

CHAPTER FIVE

JOURNEY TO JERUSALEM

Moving Under the Cloud

Eventually the ministry my husband worked for planned to move their offices to a city where it would have been difficult to travel from the settlement. We were both tired of this arduous bus ride each day, so we decided to give notice on our apartment in Ariel and move to Modiin. This is the ancient site of the Maccabees, the Jewish freedom fighters of the Chanukah story[35]. It is a beautiful city, with ample new housing. We were quite excited. For little more than what we were paying in rent for a tiny, basement, two-bedroom apartment, we could rent an entire house! A house! It seemed too good to be true. And not just any house, but a brand new house, with five bedrooms (if you include the bomb shelter, which most people just use for storage or an extra room) – and a real bathtub! After looking and looking, we found the perfect place. We prayed for God to lead and guide us, to open the right doors and close the wrong ones. We were ready to sign the deal on the house. But that open door to a five-bedroom house with a bathtub slammed shut in our faces.

---

[35] See Messiah Revealed in Chanukah book and DVD, by mail or through our website: www.voiceforisrael.com

Renting in Israel

We found out that renting a house or apartment in Israel is also not comparable to a Canadian rental experience. Rather than just driving around to find which apartment you like and signing a standard rental agreement for a month-to-month lease and moving in, renting in Israel is a complicated affair. We soon found out that rental agents require not one but two co-signers who are Israeli and have a stable paycheck, several thousands of dollars as deposit, and several months' rent up front. We were surprised they didn't ask for our first born son when we got through with the whole experience. A lawyer is also required to draft up the contract, which is usually for at least a year's lease. Legal and rental fees all add up to an enormous sum of money required to just rent, not even purchase, a place to live. It seemed impossible once again. Israel is a land where many things in the natural are impossible; a place where we come to depend entirely upon the supernatural provision and grace of God for victory.

Besides the fact that we couldn't find two co-signers, (anyone in their right mind would be crazy to co-sign for us considering our precarious financial situation), we also knew that acting as surety for someone else's debt is definitely contrary to the word of God.(Prov.6:1-2) How could we, as Bible Believers, ask someone to do something contrary to the Bible? Another kink in the hose occurred when my husband's position with the ministry began to fall apart and he was forced to resign in order to maintain his integrity before the Lord. Now we not only faced homelessness again, but also joblessness. Ah - how us baby Believers still cling to an earthly security instead of seeing ourselves as strangers and aliens on this earth and remembering that Yeshua also had no 'job' and no place to lay his head. But with a new baby and two other children, we needed a place for them at least, to lay their precious heads.

Since we no longer needed to live in Modiin, the whole

country opened up to us as a possibility and we began to seek the Lord for where He wanted to plant us. It never once occurred to us to look towards Jerusalem. We considered it too expensive, too big and too noisy, too___? We just never considered Jerusalem for a home. Our first inclination was to seek a home close to Courtney's school in order that she could live at home with the family. God provided us with the use of a car for this time, which was a major blessing, as we drove around and around this area of the country. But it seemed the same story everywhere – rents were expensive - $800 U.S. for a small 2 bedroom apartment – and the need for co-signers. At one point, we thought we had hit pay dirt! One rental agent seemed to take a shine to us and said he could find us a beautiful apartment without the need for a co-signer. We found a great apartment, not too bad as far as rents go, close to Courtney's school. We met with the owners and sat in the rental office, ready to sign on the dotted line – until we got to the part about the co-signers. Well, all right, the owner was willing to forgo this technicality – but on one condition – that we put down $4000 U.S. as a damage deposit. At this, I broke down in tears right in the office. It happened to be Yom Hashoah, Holocaust Remembrance Day, which is emotional just on its own. But we had only five days left at this point until the contract on our apartment in Ariel would expire and the new tenants would be scheduled to move in. Through my tears, I pleaded with the rental agent and owners of the apartment. I told them that we didn't have thousands of American dollars, nor did we have co-signers. I reminded them that this is the day for us to remember the tragedy of the holocaust, and that surely those survivors who made their way to Israel did not need two co-signers nor four thousand American dollars simply to find a place to lay their weary heads.

"What has happened to the people of this land?" I lamented. "Money", was their reply. It all comes down to money. "Don't you have any compassion or mercy for people trying to come home to the Land of Israel? What are we to do – live out on the street?" In fact, the newspapers did carry a story of a couple who lived on the sidewalk outside the Prime Minister's residence with their young child because they could not find a home to live. I thought, "There, but for the grace of God, go I."

In order to console ourselves, we went to a donut shop and sat discussing our options. What options? We walked around a park. We actually wandered around, calling out to God, "Baaaaaaa, baaaaaaaaaa....", reminding the Good Shepherd that His sheep are here and we are lost. *"Please come and find us"*, we pleaded, *"show us the way home."* We surrendered our own ideas of where we should live and our own agenda and schedule to the Lord of our lives. And still, every door seemed to shut in our faces, one after the other. My nose was starting to feel bloodied and sore from the impact. The day came that we had to move out of our apartment, and we still had no place to move.

We had packed everything and moved the boxes to a friend's apartment. The furniture had to go out in the backyard for the time being and we stayed on the hide-a-bed of Sheila, our good friend, neighbor and sister in the Lord across the street who had already done so much for us. It is in Sheila and Kevin's backyard that we planted our documents. It was Sheila's who washed our laundry in her own machine all those months we lived without a washing machine. She hosted ladies prayer in her home each Monday morning, and always went out of her way to make her van available to those without a car who needed a ride somewhere. One day, I'm going to feel Sheila's back for nubs from her 'angel's wings'. She and her family are not Jewish by birth, but simply obeying the call of God to live here in the Land and to bless the people of Israel. And that calling they most certainly fulfilled in our lives as well as many others. Surely, there exists a great reward awaiting people for their faithful service to the King in blessing the people of Israel.

A Divine Appointment

I wept as I packed up the last of my personal belongings into my suitcase and did a final sweep through the apartment, not knowing where we would go from here with my new baby. It was then that I remembered a message from a sister in the Lord who volunteered for the ministry where my husband had worked. Susanne also no longer worked with this ministry, but had left us her Jerusalem phone number. Not wanting to leave loose ends, I called that number and spoke with Susanne, briefly explaining our situation. *"Oh"*, she exclaimed, *"I've been working with a Messianic Rabbi from Brazil and I think he might be able to help you."* I spoke with 'Rabbi Mordechai' and to my surprise, he told me that an apartment had just come available in their building in Jerusalem and that we could come to see it if we want. Jerusalem?! Well, why not?

We knew one good thing - an elementary Messianic school existed in Jerusalem. We decided to check it out. A couple of days later we drove to Jerusalem and visited with Rabbi Mordechai and his lovely wife, Sarah. They pastored a large Messianic Congregation in Brazil under the covering of the Consoler Center of Israel. Sarah was a well-known Christian singer in Brazil and had cut her own CD called Sh'ma Israel. Despite their high-profile as Christians in Brazil, they had no problems whatsoever making Aliyah in 1998.[36] Because of the rising anti-Semitism in South American countries, many new immigrants are coming from these areas and are therefore not suspected as Believers.

Mordechai introduced us to the owner of the apartment, who gave us the quick tour. Despite being smaller than we had originally hoped for and up several flights of stairs with

---

36 Unfortunately, Sarah and Mordechai left the land to pastor a church in the U.S. and later their marriage broke apart through tragic circumstances.

no elevator, we were prepared by now to squish and sweat for the sake of just having a place to live in this Land. Did we need a co-signer? No, the landlady said that Mordechai's recommendation of us was enough. Even Mordechai was going on blind faith, wanting to help a brother and sister in the Lord. In fact, their calling in the land was just to help, comfort, and console that people of Israel. Did we need a huge deposit? No, just one month's rent was enough. We couldn't believe it! Looking for that inevitable snag, we asked, *"Do we need to give you several months rent in advance?"* *"No"*, she said, *"one month at a time would be fine."* Now this was truly too good to be true. God was bringing us, not only to His Land, but to His holy eternal city Jerusalem the place where His temple once stood, where He promised to place His name forever, and where He will one day return to establish His eternal kingdom. This was truly more than we could expect or imagine that God would do for us.

> **"Now to Him who is able to do immeasurably more than all we ask or imagine, according to his power that is at work within us, to Him be glory in the Church and in Messiah Yeshua throughout all generations, forever and ever! Amen!"** (Eph. 3:20)

We checked out the Messianic School, Makor Hatikvah, for our seven year old son, Timothy (Shmuel) and spoke with the principal. One of the first things he made clear was the prohibition in the school against violence. Children in this school are not allowed to beat each other up, as is unfortunately so common in Israeli public elementary schools. Violence is becoming a serious problem in Israeli schools. Even Liat experienced it in gan (kindergarten). Here was her wise beyond her years perspective:

Day 1:
Mom: *"Liat, how was gan?"*
Liat: *"Well, there are bad kids there who bother me."*
Mom: *"Can you keep away from the bad kids?"*
Liat: *"Oh yes, I can run!!"*

Day 2:
Mom: *"Liat, how was gan today?"*
Liat: *"Well, the kids were still bad, but I punched them in the face!"*
Mom: *"Oh dear, Liat. You know, you could pray instead."*
Liat: *"I did pray, Mom, and God told me to punch them in the face!"*
    Kids say the funniest things! ☺

    Forty rambunctious children in a classroom with one harassed and overworked teacher, combined with slack home discipline and a violent environment in general is a recipe for disaster. It grieved my heart that my young son had to endure this kind of schooling in Ariel. When the children came to school dressed as witches, goblins, and vampires for the festival of Purim, we finally pulled him out of the school and searched for alternatives. This small, private school seemed the only alternative for Timothy and it has been a great blessing to have the privilege of sending him to a school in Jerusalem where they start their day with a prayer meeting and teach the whole Bible (Old and New Testaments).[37] At the time that Timothy attended Makor Hatikvah, the school struggled to stay alive. Often, the teachers went for months without being paid their basic salary until the money trickled in by God's grace and a lot of fasting and prayer on the part of staff and parents. Over the past several years, however, the school has experienced tremendous growth and expansion. They are now discussing the possibility of opening more

---

37 Makor Hatikvah, meaning source of hope, is one of only two Messianic schools in Israel. To contact: PO Box 2793, Jerusalem 91027

Messianic schools in other parts of the country. PTL!

We became very good friends with another couple, Colin & Rosie, trying to make aliyah from England, who also had enrolled their children in Makor Hatikvah. Our children and theirs also became fast friends and so the Lord sent people to fellowship and share our lives with. Much of Colin's family had been killed in the Holocaust, but because of Colin's faith in Yeshua, the Israeli government was also denying his citizenship. Rosie formed the Gentile half of the 'one new man' marriage and was equally committed to live in the Land of Israel and to raise their children there. So often, they would get a letter ordering them to leave the country, but Colin would always say if they were Jewish enough for the Nazis to murder them, then they are Jewish enough to live in the Land of Israel. As well as prayer and intercession, they hired lawyers to fight the legal battle and they won the right to reside in the Land. I admire so much their determination, courage and perseverance in fighting the good fight of faith. They simply refused to stop believing and refused to give up. I remember them coming to our place and singing the words of the prophets that God would plant them in this land, never to be pulled up from the land God has given us. And in the end, they obtained the victory! They are now active in the Hebrew speaking congregation, and Colin is now the Vice Principal of this school. Halleluyah!

Welcome to the Family

As our individual family grew and adjusted to living in Jerusalem, we needed to find a place where we could belong as part of the larger family of God, the Body of Messiah in Jerusalem. Although several Messianic congregations exist in Jerusalem, we had yet to find one that felt like a 'fit' for us. One of Timothy's teachers, a lovely young woman named

Tikvah, would often mention a particular congregation, which somehow resonated with my spirit. I determined one week to attend their service, only to find that I came down with a fever the afternoon prior. Never mind, I thought, I will go next week, but when the next time came, the same thing happened. I began to feel ill and perspire with a high fever. The third time it happened, recognizing it to be a diversion from the enemy, I said to myself, "I don't care – I'm going!" I took the bus, feeling nauseous and perspiring profusely, and searched for the congregation in downtown Jerusalem. Here, we cannot find the places by looking them up in the phone book. They can't advertise! Nor will there be a big sign out front announcing its location, lest the religious storm the building or burn it down. I had no idea, actually, how I would find it, but I walked down a back alley and saw a person standing there whom the Holy Spirit showed me was a Believer. Sure enough, it was someone from the congregation, and I stood just outside the building. She led me inside and through a thick, metal bomb shelter door which closed and locked behind me. I followed the sound of the beautiful worship music to a large room which held the services. In front of me hung a huge banner with the words:

אני יהוה רפאך
I am the Lord who heals you.

I knew I had come to the right place. People were kind to me, handing me Kleenexes to wipe my tears and hugs to wash away my fears. After the service, as I prepared to leave, someone approached me with a message from the pastor that he wanted to have a word with me in his office. There, I met the congregational leader who had preached such a powerful message. Commanding the presence of the Lord like a general, with the anointing still resting upon him, Shimon said that the Holy Spirit pointed me out to him and said that it was very important that I had come to their

Kehilla. Shimon then personally welcomed me into his 'family'. Little did he know that, within a year's time, we truly would become family, as his son, Emanuel, and my daughter, Courtney sealed their 'betrothal' with the wine and bread of covenant in that very place, with Shimon one year later, officiating at their wedding. Halleluyah!

LOVE AT FIRST SIGHT

It was love at first sight on Shavuot (Pentecost) when they first met at a congregational picnic at Gan Hashosha (The Third Garden), one of the most beautiful and romantic places in all of Israel, with orchids overhanging natural pools and streams and waterfalls. Courtney had spent hours making her famous 'Shavuot cheesecake' from scratch. [38] We actually caught the moment on videotape when she served a slice to Emanuel. He took it from her hands with a smile and said, "Oh, Courtney, you are a sweetheart!" The wind whipped Courtney's long hair and threatened to blow the cake away, but they had eyes only for each other. Later, we showed this video clip at their wedding and laughed. But actually, Courtney had her eye on Emanuel even before this – she first saw him when I brought her to the congregation one weekend that she visited home from her boarding school. I could see her watching this beautiful, blonde young man worship the Lord on the platform. He looked more like a movie star or actor than a worship leader, but it was his inner beauty and pure love for the Lord that was so compelling. Courtney leaned over and whispered in my ear, "Mom, he sings like an angel!" Indeed, he does sing with the voice of an angel. In my heart, I thought like a Jewish mother, "Wouldn't he make a wonderful husband for my precious daughter?!" But it almost seemed too much to even dare hope for – out of the realm of possibilities. My Cinderella

---

38 Cheesecake, blintzes, and other dairy products are traditional foods served on Shavuot (Festival of Weeks/Pentecost).

girl from a commoner family marrying 'a prince'? Surely, I thought, a young man like this must have young women lined up, waiting for a chance to date the son of the pastor! It was to my great surprise, then, to find out that his life was his music and to this point, he had not even kissed a girl, let alone had a serious relationship. When his mother, Batya, asked me about Courtney, and found out that she too had committed at a young age to 'true love waits', we were both thrilled that our children had kept themselves pure for marriage according to God's holy standards. At the age of twelve, at her Bat Mitzvah, (a Jewish coming of age ceremony for a girl), I had given Courtney a heart-shaped necklace with the words, True Love Waits - her 'covenant necklace'. Wearing it was her pledge that she would wait and keep herself sexually pure for the one man that God intended to be her husband. All her friends witnessed her pledge and signed their names to the True Love Waits card; it was a powerful ceremony. One of the most precious moments of my life was when my beautiful daughter, just moments before walking up the aisle to meet her bridegroom, turned to me and, taking off her necklace, placed it lovingly in my hands saying, "You keep this for me now, Mom, I won't be needing it anymore."

Shira Sorko-Ram wrote an article about their wedding in the Maoz Israel Report (July 2002). The following is an excerpt from her article:

"Being the romanticist that he is, he (Emanuel) decided that he was going to have a wedding to end all weddings, which he himself meticulously planned out. He selected the setting for their spring wedding in an outdoor restaurant overlooking Jerusalem on a hill called Armon Hanatsiv. There is a beautiful walkway along the length of the hill, and it overlooks, perhaps, the most beautiful view in all of Israel,...The only negative aspect is that this hill is isolated with bushes and trees and there are no other immediate buildings except for this one restaurant. It had

only been a few weeks prior that a couple strolling along this walkway had been attacked by a terrorist and the woman was stabbed to death. The wedding was to be at night and with all Israel's security forces doing their best. There had, nevertheless, been 60 suicide attacks over the last 18 months..."

From Hannah: I received a call mid-morning from Courtney, crying, telling me that the wedding will have to be cancelled. A fierce wind began to blow early that morning and had blown down the tent covering and all the decorations, completely ruining them. The forecast said that the winds would continue all day and the wedding was scheduled to begin in less than 10 hours. We prayed for a miracle and in a short while, Courtney phoned back with a praise report – they had miraculously managed to find a wedding hall at the last minute and were transferring the entire wedding to this indoor location, an auditorium complex in Jerusalem. This was a far more secure location than Armon HaNatsiv.

At 4:20 in the afternoon, Courtney and I sat in a beauty salon in downtown Jerusalem, getting 'beautified' for the wedding. Courtney insisted that I also have someone professionally set my hair and do my makeup. Courtney looked absolutely stunning in her wedding gown, which had been generously lent to us by the International Christian Embassy of Jerusalem (ICEJ). Even choosing the wedding dress turned out to be a supernatural event. The woman in charge of this bridal ministry initially refused to let Courtney look at their selection of hundreds upon hundreds of dresses, saying that it would take hours or even days to find the right dress and since it was Friday, they would be closing early in preparation for Shabbat (the Sabbath).[39] But Courtney

---

39 In Israel, everything shuts down early on Friday afternoons to prepare for a total shut down of business for the holy seventh day Sabbath. Buses also stop running and in religious sections of Israel, even cars are not allowed to drive on their streets. It is a beautiful, peaceful, restful day for everyone in the nation (except emergency personnel).

pleaded with her and who can resist such a smile? So she gave her just five minutes. And in that five minutes, Courtney went directly to the rack, pulled out one dress, tried it on and this was her perfect wedding dress! Perfect style and fit! As it turned out, the woman at the ICEJ bridal shop turned out to be our close neighbor. She and her husband, Americans volunteering with ICEJ, became two of our very good friends in Jerusalem.

As the Bride- to-be, mother of the bride and future mother in law sat in the beauty salon, we were jolted almost out of our seats by a deafening blast. Just a few minutes later, the radio began to report that another suicide bomber had detonated himself in downtown Jerusalem, very close to the salon, killing three people and wounding 87. The day before another terrorist had killed three and wounded 60 others just a few stores away. The owner of the salon hollered, Turn that radio off! There are brides in here and they don't want to hear about this on their wedding day!" Such is life in Israel – it goes on – people continue to marry and have parties and give birth to children, all against a backdrop of terror and violence.

Shira: *"The wedding was gorgeous. The beautiful music had been composed and recorded by Emanuel for his bride. In my opinion, it compared with anything Hollywood could have produced. Everyone wondered how such a beautiful wedding ...with lights, sound effects, and even fireworks (outside the windows) could have been fashioned in just a few short hours at the new location. We, of course, could not forget that we were in Jerusalem; under the purple-violet lighting were eight armed guards, one with a ready machine gun...*

Hannah: One of the guests at the wedding, now doing his military service on the police force in Jerusalem confided that the suicide bomber who had blown himself up that afternoon downtown was the one that Israeli Police were looking for all morning. They knew he was planning a suicide bombing in Israel and he had been arrested but had escaped from jail. Police had been looking for him in the Talpiot area which borders Armon HaNatsiv, the original site of where the wedding was going to take place. An Arab village right across the valley from this location could likely see all the wedding decorations going up, so the terrorist could have been hiding in the bushes waiting for the evening to come. Weddings and other joyous occasions and festivals are favorite targets of suicide bombers in Israel. What the police know is that, in mid-afternoon of the day of the wedding, the terrorist boarded a bus at the Armon HaNatsiv bus stop by the restaurant and exploded himself downtown a short time later. Quite likely he saw all the decorations and the tent covering blown down and knew the wedding guests would not arrive so he changed his plans.

What is amazing to me is that even though we prayed and cried out for the wind and rain and storm to stop, God knows better. It was such a powerful lesson in trust and surrender for all of us, to know that sometimes the storms and the changes and interruptions and delays are not simply to frustrate us, but to protect us and to show us God's love and care. I believe it was the Lord who sent the wind to blow down the tent to force a move to a location of safety. God is so good! Especially when he sometimes says 'no' and holds his ground despite our pleading and begging for a yes. The question is, "Will we trust Him?"

Voice of the Bride and the Bridegroom

One of the worst judgments God inflicted upon Israel during the time of her punishment was the loss of the voices of the Bridegroom and the Bride: "**Moreover I will take from them the voice of joy and the voice of gladness, the voice of the bridegroom and the voice of the bride…and this whole land shall be a desolation…** (Jer. 25:10-11) But

God never leaves us without hope of restoration – the turning of sorrow to joy, of mourning to dancing. He promised that one day the punishment would end and the land would once again here these joyous sounds: **"Thus says the Lord: Again there shall be heard in this place …the voice of joy and the voice of gladness, the voice of the bridegroom and the voice of the bride …" (Jer. 33:10-11)** How wonderful it was to personally participate in this restoration of the favor of God upon Zion.

Courtney and Emanuel's wedding was not just a beautiful wedding in the natural of two special people joining their lives together forever; not just a testimony to sexual purity for youth and singles; it was a visual and auditory prophetic act. The strident call of the shofar, the regal entrance of the Bridegroom, the gazes of adoration as the Bride encircled her Beloved seven times according to Jewish wedding customs, symbolizing an ever deepening walk into his soul, the free and spontaneous dancing of the Bride and the Bridegroom, finally one, abandoning themselves to love; even the wedding feast – it all gave us the unforgettable taste of how wonderful it will be when the Messiah comes for us - His Beloved Bride. "Ani l'dodi, v'dodi li" I am my beloved's and my beloved is mine. Forever. (Song of Songs 6:3) Perhaps their wedding also stands as a testament to God's protective power to keep us, even in times of danger, until that day. Until we stand under the Chuppah, the wedding canopy, with our Beloved. For we are children of God and the evil one cannot touch us as we dwell in the secret place of Elyon, under the shade of Shaddai, covered by the shelter of His wings (Psalm 91).

Now their son, Adden, is being raised as a third generation Jewish Israeli Believer in Jerusalem. Halleluyah! (Courtney and Emanuel should soon have a website up where you can read their vision for worship in Israel. To contact them, write to them at Box 2772, Jerusalem 91023, Israel. To receive a copy of their wedding DVD, <u>A Messianic</u>

Jewish wedding in Jerusalem, please contact us by mail or through our website: www.voiceforisrael.com

Courtney, Emanuel, and their son, Adden

CHAPTER SIX

GOD'S PLAN FOR THE JEWISH PEOPLE IN THE DIASPORA: TO COME HOME

> "For I am God, and there is no other; I am God, and there is none like Me, ... My counsel shall stand, and I will do all My pleasure... Indeed I have spoken it; I will also bring it to pass. I have purposed it; I will also do it."
> (Is. 46:11)

An Urgent Appeal For Aliyah

Most Jewish people reading this book would probably consider that the prospect of making Aliyah, of immigrating to Israel, at this point in time would have to be meshuganah (crazy, insane, out of one's mind). Yes, according to what we can see with our natural eyes, it would most definitely be craziness or insanity to want to move from one's nice, safe, comfortable home, leaving all friends and family behind, spending a lot of money and putting up with a great deal of inconvenience, to move to Israel. And this holds true, especially now with all the reported violence and unrest in the country. So why do it? I can think of one main positive reason, and one main negative one. These are not trivial or light responses – they may be matters of life or death for the Jewish people.

Time of Jacob's Trouble

We "People of the Book", are not to live by sight alone, but also by faith and by the Word of God. We assert, in our principles of faith, that every word of the prophets are true. If we really believe what we believe, then we know that a terrible time of trouble will come upon the earth. One day, and possibly soon according to all the signs of growing trouble, chaos, and violence in the world, God is going to settle accounts. He is coming to judge the world. When he does come with vengeance and with judgment, there may be no safe place for the Jewish people except within the land of Israel. The prophet Jeremiah speaks of a terrible time called the time of 'Jacob's trouble'.

> **"Cries of fear are heard – terror, not peace. Ask and see: Can a man bear children? Then why do I see every strong man with his hands on his stomach like a woman in labor, every face turned deathly pale? How awful that day will be! None will be like it. It will be a <u>time of trouble for Jacob</u>, but he will be saved out of it."** (Jer. 30:4-7)

How will God save Jacob (the children of Israel) out of this awful time? By bringing them back into the Land, God has provided a place of refuge for His people.

> **"So do not fear, O Jacob my servant; do not be dismayed, O Israel, I will surely save you out of a distant place, your descendants from the land of their exile. Jacob will again have**

peace and security, and no one will make him afraid. I am with you and will save you," (Jer. 30:10-11)

Why do Jewish people in the diaspora seriously need to consider getting out of their lands of exile? Because God's judgment is soon to fall upon these nations:

"Though I completely destroy all the nations among which I scatter you, I will not completely destroy you." (Jer. 30:11b)

The Jewish people will not go completely unpunished when God's judgment falls upon the nations; they will be disciplined with justice. But He will have mercy upon His children. He will send all Israel's enemies into exile and instead, will bring those Jews left in exile back to their own land. It is here in the Land, that God will restore our health and heal our wounds; He will restore our fortunes, have compassion on us, bring us honor and joy, establish our community and punish all who oppress us. These are God's great and wonderful promises towards His people Israel in the Land.

Listen to more scriptures from our own Hebrew prophets and see if you may not agree that, although it looks like Israel is besieged and oppressed by the enemy here in Israel (God is going to fight for us here in the land and protect us. He gives no such assurance in the land of our exile, since this is the place of punishment, not of blessing. For Jewish people to remain in exile even though God has re-birthed the nation of Israel and opened its doors to our return, is to profane His Holy name.

"And wherever they went among the nations they profaned my holy name, for it was said

of them, 'These are the Lord's people, and yet they had to leave His land.'" (Ezek. 36:20)

It is not for our sakes, the Lord says, that He is bringing us home but for the sake of His reputation as the God of Israel.

> "Thus says the Lord God: 'I do not do this for your sake, O house of Israel, but for my holy name's sake which you have profaned among the nations wherever you went." (Ezekiel 36:22)

To come home to our own land is therefore to sanctify His holy name among the nations of the world.

What will happen to the Jews who remain in exile when God destroys the nations? Well, of course there is only One who knows the answers for certain, but if we study the prophetic word, we will see that God will bring many back to the Land through passing under the bond of His covenant, but not all will make it back to the Land. Those who revolt and rebel against God will be purged from the nation through judgment.

> "I will take note of you as you pass under my rod, and I will bring you into the bond of the covenant. I will purge you of those who revolt and rebel against me. Although I will bring them out of the land where they are living, yet they will not enter the land of Israel." (Ezek. 20:37, 38)

This is a strong warning to the Jews who stubbornly hold onto their lives of earthly security and comfort in the Diaspora, the lands of their exile. Once the persecution hits, it may be too late to get back to the Land. Chuck, a

Messianic pastor here in Jerusalem once tried to fly from Israel to North America with his children, but when he got to the airport, they were stopped. The children's passports had expired and they could not make it out of the country. They had to return home. Their neighbor, Ted, who was at that time president of the pro-life Israel ministry, saw them returning home in the middle of the night and came to see what was wrong. Ted brought Chuck and his family over for dinner, straightened out the bureaucratic red tape for the children's passports, and paid for their taxi back to the airport. The next day, they were happily on their way to visit grandma and grandpa in America. But Chuck could not shake this terrible feeling of dread and fear that hung over him and during the flight, He prayed and asked the Lord to reveal the source of his feelings, which were entirely disproportionate to the situation. The Lord revealed to him that this would be the same situation but in reverse when the Jews want to leave America. Many will be turned back at the airport and not able to make it to the refuge of the Land, where the Jews in Israel have been beckoning them for over fifty years now. It will only be through people like Ted, Christians who love the Jewish people and devote their lives to them, who will give food, shelter, and financial assistance to get them out of the country. The Spirit of God has been directing people to prepare 'safe houses' across the nations, and especially across Europe for many years now. They are awaiting the Exodus to begin and for the Jews to come.

If we look at God bringing Israel out of Egypt, we see that even in the midst of the plagues, God did protect his covenant people. But note – it was only through their faith in the blood of the lamb, and their application of this blood to their doorposts that they were saved. If they had not applied the blood to their doorposts, their firstborns would have perished just like the Egyptians. What is the bond of the covenant which all must pass under? It is the new covenant sealed in the blood of the Lamb of God, Yeshua the Messiah. Please give this matter your utmost consideration and make it a matter of serious prayer to our God – the God of Abraham, Isaac, and Jacob, for we are forbidden to pray to anyone but Him. Ask Him to show you the way to a relationship of peace and forgiveness with Him; ask Him to reveal to you the Truth about the blood of the lamb. I urge you to place your faith in our God, and in obedience to Him, trust in the way of salvation that He has provided for you by sacrificing His son, Yeshua, to atone for all of our sins. He is called the Lamb of God. By faith, place this blood upon the lintels of your heart, knowing that the power of this blood, along with your faith and trust in God, will save you from His soon coming wrath.

Mrs. Hannah Newman, author of an article on the dangers of the New Age movement and Jewish people offers ALIYAH as one appropriate response to this threat. This is a quote from her article: Accelerate the Gathering of Diaspora Jews to Israel.

"It is obvious now more than ever that the Jews have no way of defending themselves outside the Land. When the Global Governance system becomes operational, it will be international policy to discriminate against Jews, to take away their children who have been "wrongly indoctrinated" and to target the whole lot of us for "cleansing action".

The only defensible position for Jews of any persuasion is to stand with their own people in their own land, where we have survived enemy attacks time and again (though rationally we can't explain why...). It is also the best defensive policy for Israel -- the more the better, since even with God's help, **"Five will chase one hundred but a hundred will chase ten thousand."** (Lev. 26:8)

According to the published N.A. (new age) timetable, this leaves world Jewry about one to three years to consolidate in their land before they may be faced with the "Luciferic initiation" or the alternative. (God may decide to postpone their Plan again as He has apparently done several times, but who wants to gamble on this chance with their family?)

One of the best reasons to live in the Land is because it is a mitzvah (a commandment). An Israeli, Orthodox Jewish writer who prefers to remain anonymous wrote the following letter.

THE COMMANDMENT TO LIVE IN THE LAND

The Real Peace Process, February 26, 2001

There are Jews who meticulously observe the commandments, even to the point of going beyond what is required. Just plain kosher isn't enough, they must have only glatt kosher. On Succot they will spend hours choosing the most beautiful etrog[40] and spend extra money to glorify the mitzvah[41]. And, on Passover, they will only eat Matzah Shmurah.[42] Yet, when it comes to one mitzvah which is as

---

40 Etrog is a small lemon like fruit used in the celebration of sukkot, feast of tabernacles.
41 Mitzvah – commandment or good deed.
42 A Specially baked Matzah, unleavened bread, for Passover.

important as all the mitzvot[43] combined, the mitzvah to settle in the Land of Israel, these same observant Jews seek to avoid this particular mitzvah and stake their lack of observance upon minority opinions.

They will tell you that the state of Israel today is not an observant state. There is even a large anti-religious element there. What they choose not to think about is the rabbinical mandate, which states that it is better to live in Eretz Yisrael[44] among a majority of goyim[45], than to live in the exile among a majority of observant Jews. They choose not to think about the concept that one who lives in the exile is as one who has no God. They choose not to consider that the very fact that Jews continue to live in exile is a desecration of God. This has always been the case, but how much more so today, when we have a sovereign Jewish State in the Land of Israel? Plainly stated it is a sin for a Jew to willfully remain in the exile when he can live in the Land of Israel, even as it is today.

Of course we must all strive to improve ourselves and come closer to His Torah. It is true that the Jewish State today is far from what we would like it to be. While it certainly is a mitzvah to yearn for the coming of the Messiah and complete redemption, that is not license to sit on our hands and just wait for God to do everything. We must earn a speedy and glorious redemption by expressing our faith in God. Faith means a lot more than words. It means that we must be prepared to sacrifice for our beliefs. While perhaps prior to 1948 arguments could be made that it was not the right time for us to rebuild our homeland, certainly the very fact that it has been successfully acquired by our people (secular or otherwise) refutes such arguments. A Jew

---

43 Plural for mitzvah.
44 Eretz yisrael – the land of Israel.
45 Goyim - Gentiles.

of true faith understands that if it were not the Will of God for the Jewish State to be rebuilt, then it simply would not have been rebuilt. No amount of physical might can change the Will of God.

The reason that we have problems with Arabs is simply because our own leaders have never been able to accept the fact that Zionism is a Godly process. Had they been able to understand this reality they certainly would have understood that we have no right to try to negotiate our destiny. Had our leaders recognized the magnitude of the Divine Process of Jewish Redemption, they would at least have had the courage to stand up to the challenge with the same obstinacy that enabled our Arab neighbors to declare, "Not One Inch." Had this been our national policy from the outset the redemption certainly would have been hastened. It was clearly as a direct result of our placing our fear of man above our fear of God that has caused us these problems.

How can I blame Arafat for murdering Jews after my own government gave him money, guns, ammunition, training, and bases within Israel from which to launch attacks against us? Did they really think that Arafat would use these things to protect us?

Redemption will only come through Jewish faith in God. One of the best ways for a Jew to express that faith is for him to leave the "safe" exile, and come home to live in "dangerous" Israel. The Arabs are not the problem. It is our refusal to accept our Divine role which brings needless tragedy upon us. Of course we must return to our Jewish roots, and to the Jewish way of life. But this clearly includes return to the Jewish homeland with pride and self-respect. The only place in the world where the mitzvot of the Torah have any significance is in the Land of Israel. Jews who do mitzvot yet choose to live outside of the Land cannot claim complete Torah observance.

Yes it is dangerous in Israel today. Yes we have terrible problems within our own society, even aside from the threats from our enemies. It is true that Messiah is not yet here and the redemption is not yet complete. But all of these things really should encourage us rather than discourage us. How could we possibly express our faith in God were He to suddenly transform the Jewish State into a fully observant one and turn all of us into absolute angels? He already has angels. Angels do not have the ability to choose between right and wrong; good and evil. They also cannot exhibit faith for that reason. This is what enables Man to raise himself even above angels.

God has given us enough evidence to see that He is in control. Now, all we have to do is trust in Him and sanctify His Holy Name with our deeds. When a Jew leaves a pleasant exile and chooses to live in a "dangerous" Israel because he knows that this is God's will, that is sanctification of our God. And when a Jewish government, even a secular one, tells the Arab nations and even the President of the United States that it is forbidden by God for a Jewish government to part with any Jewish Land and that the concept of territories for peace will only work if Jewish territories are returned to the Jewish people and not the other way around, then we will see a real peace process.

I think this says it better than I ever could. One of the main reasons for making Aliyah is simply this – it is a mitzvah (a commandment).

You Can Catch More Bees with Honey

On the more positive side, the Word of God contains many, many magnificent and wonderful promises for those who do have the chutzpah (nerve) to make Aliyah. God promises to restore all things to us in the Land– to restore our fortunes, our health, our peace, our relationship with Him, through Yeshua. My dad always used to say: "You can catch more bees with honey than vinegar…"

Once again, we must live not by sight alone, but by faith. Yes, I realize that many people in Israel are struggling. But God's promises for blessing us here in the land are conditional – they are IF we keep His Torah here and obey His commandments – IF we do what is right in His sight, seek after justice, righteousness, and walk humbly with our God – IF we give to the poor in the land and don't shut our ears to their cries.

I am not encouraging you to follow the form of Orthodox Rabbinic Judaism as practiced in the Land today with all their myriads of man-made rules and regulations.

No, you don't have to pre-rip your toilet paper in the bathroom, or leave the food on 'warm' all night. These rules were created and designed by human precept and constitute a large part of our Jewish tradition. But in order to enjoy the full blessings promised to us in the Land, we need to return to God and His written word in the Torah, and to find peace with God through the atonement He has provide us through the Messiah, the Savior of the World, Yeshua.

This is a word the Lord gave through the prophet Jeremiah to the Jews who wanted to live outside the Land of Israel because they feared the dangers. God said that everything they feared about living in the Land would actually come upon them in the land they considered 'safe'. We can make a big mistake trying to play it safe through life: [46]

> "If you will still remain in this land, then I will build you and not pull you down, and I will plant you and not pluck you up...But if you say, 'We will not dwell in this land,' disobeying the voice of the Lord your God, saying, 'No, but we will go to the land of Egypt where we shall see no war, nor hear the sound of the trumpet, nor be hungry for bread, and there we will dwell – then hear now the word of the Lord, O remnant of Judah! Thus says the Lord of Hosts, the God of Israel: 'If you wholly set your faces to enter Egypt, and go to dwell there, then it shall be that the sword which you feared shall overtake you there in the land of Egypt; the famine of which you were afraid shall follow close after you there in Egypt; and there you shall die." (Jer. 42:10, 13-16)

---

46 See article archives, "Living as a Sukkah – Playing it Safe" www.voiceforisrael.com

CHAPTER SEVEN

GOD'S PLAN FOR ISRAEL: OUR GOD WILL SAVE US!

Today looks like a dark, bleak day for the people of Israel. Many Israelis are reaching the point of despair. But in order to see from God's perspective, we need to look at His prophetic word. Israel's future and destiny is glory, honor, and salvation.

God has a covenant with Israel, which is unbroken, since God is a covenant keeper. Within this land and this city will one day be peace (shalom) and praise.

> **"Look upon Zion, the city of our festivals; your eyes will see Jerusalem, a peaceful abode, a tent that will not be moved; its stakes will never be pulled up nor any of its ropes broken. There the Lord will be our Mighty One...For the Lord is our judge, the Lord is our lawgiver, the Lord is our king; it is he who will save us..."** (Is. 33:20-22)

Healing and divine forgiveness will be found here:

> "No one living in Zion will say, 'I am ill' and the sins of those who dwell there will be forgiven." (Is. 33:20-24)

God will be reconciled once again with His people and bring them home again:

> "The Lord will have compassion on Jacob, once again he will choose Israel and will settle them in their own land." (Is. 14:1)

The land of Israel will be a place of refuge:

> "The Lord has established Zion, and in her his afflicted people will find refuge." (Is. 14:32)

The Lord will answer the cries of His people when they cry out to Him:

> "O people of Zion, who live in Jerusalem, you will weep no more. How gracious He will be when you cry for help! As soon as he hears, he will answer you." (Is. 30:19)

One day, Israel will experience an even more glorious Passover than in Egypt:

> "...so the Lord Almighty will come down to do battle on Mount Zion and on its heights. Like birds hovering overhead, the Lord Almighty will shield Jerusalem; he will shield it and deliver it. He will 'pass over' it and will rescue it." (Is. 31:4, 5)

God has chosen Israel, called her children home to the Land, set her apart for His service, and will not reject her.

God will strengthen us and help us. We need not fear:

> "But you, O Israel, my servant, Jacob, whom I have chosen, you descendants of Abraham, my friend. I took you from the ends of the earth, from the farthest corners I called you. I said, You are my servant; I have chosen you and have not rejected you. So do not fear, for I am with you, do not be dismayed, for I am your God. I will strengthen you and help you; I will uphold you with my righteous right hand." (Is. 41:8-10)

God will destroy all of Israel's enemies:

> "All who rage against you will surely be ashamed and disgraced; those who oppose you will be as nothing and perish. Though you search for your enemies, you will not find them. Those who wage war against you will be as nothing at all." (Is. 41:11-12)

Israel is tiny, but God is great; we need not fear:

> " For I am the Lord your God, who takes hold of your right hand and says to you, Do not fear; I will help you, Do not be afraid, O worm Jacob, O little Israel, for I myself will help you, declares the Lord, your Redeemer, the Holy One of Israel." (Is. 41:14)

Israel belongs to God and will protect what is His:

> "Fear not, for I have redeemed you; I have summoned you by name, you are mine. When you pass through the waters, I will be with you; and when you pass through the

> rivers, they will not sweep over you. When you walk through the fire, you will not be burned, the flames will not set you ablaze. For I am the Lord your God, the Holy one of Israel, your Savior." (Is. 43:1-3)

For a time, it may seem that God has forsaken Zion, but He will never forget her. She is engraved on the palms of God's hands:

> "But Zion said, 'The Lord has forsaken me, the Lord has forgotten me.' Can a mother forget the baby at her breast and have no compassion on the child she has borne? Though she may forget, I will never forget you! See, I have engraved you on the palms of my hands; your walls are ever before me." (Is. 49:14-16)

These are God's words and if He has said it, we may be assured that He will also bring it to pass. God is God and His purposes will stand:

> "I am God, and there is no other; I am God, and there is none like me...I say: My purpose will stand and I will do all that I please...What I have said, that will I bring about; what I have planned, that will I do." (Is. 46:9-11)

What is it exactly that He promises to do for Israel?

> "I will grant salvation to Zion, my splendor to Israel." (Is. 46:13)

Spiritual Salvation

The salvation that God has planned for Israel includes not only the physical salvation of the nation, but also its spiritual salvation. The prophet Ezekiel describes this miracle in chapter 37. The Lord commanded the prophet to prophesy to the dry bones, which represented the whole house of Israel. Even though there was no breath in them, Ezekiel prophesied as commanded and the breath (Spirit) entered the dry bones so that they came to life and stood up on their feet – a vast army. Pictures of the holocaust show in grisly detail, the mounds of dry bones, which were the only remains of so many Jews, murdered by the Nazis. The people of Israel said,

> **"Our hope is gone; we are cut off (from God's covenant of mercy)."** (Ezek. 37:11)

Today, many people in Israel feel the same way – that their hope is gone; that they are cut off from God and alone in the world as all the nations seem to be turning against them. Internal division and civil strife plagues the country as much as the Arab terrorists in our midst. Recently, a Jerusalem hall collapsed, killing several members of a wedding party and injuring over a hundred others who were crushed under the debris. Following on the heels of this tragedy, a Palestinian suicide bomber blew himself up at a Tel Aviv disco, killing twenty teenagers, most of them Russian immigrants, and injuring many other young teens. Most recently, a five-month old baby lost consciousness after being hit in the head by a Palestinian's stone that smashed through the windshield of the family's car. Two days ago the baby died.

If God loves Israel so much, why is this happening? Why is Israel not able to stand against her enemies? It is because even more than God cares about His people's physical, temporary lives here on earth, He cares deeply about our eternal souls. In order for God to grant us spiritual salvation, He must first deal with our sins.

The Sin of Achan

Most Jewish people, both inside and outside Israel, have lost much of their 'sin consciousness'. Due to their lack of a sound scriptural foundation, they simply do not know what constitutes 'sin' in God's sight. But in this case, ignorance is not bliss, for God is a holy judge who must punish sin, whether the people are aware of their sin or not. One Biblical case in point is the sin of Achan. When Joshua and his army of men took the city of Jericho, God gave them strict instructions to 'abstain from the accursed things'. Jericho, as the first fruits of Israel's conquest of the land was doomed to destruction, as were all in it, except for Rahab the Harlot and her family, since she helped the Israelite spies. God warned them not to take anything from Jericho, lest they bring a curse upon the camp of Israel.

> **"But Achan, ...of the tribe of Judah, took of the accursed things; so the anger of the Lord burned against the children of Israel."**
> (Josh. 7:1)

After spying on the people of Ai, their next conquest, they advised Joshua that only about two or three thousand men would be necessary to defeat the people of Ai, for they were few in number. This was definitely not a formidable foe. And yet, Israel came running back crying, with their tale between their legs, having suffered a sound defeat.

> **"Therefore the hearts of the people melted and became like water."** (Josh. 7:5)

Joshua was so discouraged, he tore his clothes and fell on his face before the Lord, crying, "Why did you bring this people to cross the Jordan – only to deliver us into the hands of our enemies? Why did we ever come here? Why couldn't we just have been content to stay on the other side of the Jordan?" This is the spirit of many of the people in Israel today when they see that God is delivering them into the hands of their enemies. Some are even questioning why they even came to the Land. Most people think we are out of our minds to have come here from Canada, but this gives us the opening we need to share from God's prophetic word. Joshua asks God what message to give to the people of Israel.

> **"O Lord, what shall I say when Israel turns its back before its enemies?"** (v. 8)

In Israel today, it seems as if both the Barak government and the current Sharon government simply turns its back before its enemies, allowing them to shoot and stone and blow up whichever Israeli citizen they please. God had an answer for Joshua and He has an answer for us today:

> **"Get up! Why do you lie thus on your face? Israel has sinned, and they have also transgressed My covenant which I commanded them."** (Josh. 7:10)

There it is – Israel has sinned and broken their covenant with their God. Israel could not then and will not today stand against her enemies until they purge the camp of sin. God tolerated sin in His newborn nation and defended her for a time on the basis of His reputation, but the time is coming to call His people to account. Judgment starts with the House of God – it will then extend to all the nations.

> "Surely He is God who judges in the earth."
> (Ps. 58:11)

Covenants – Blessing and Cursing

Israel faces a choice today, as they have for centuries – to obey God and enjoy His blessings, or disobey and suffer His curses.

> **"See, I am setting before you today a blessing and a curse ..."** (Deut. 11:26)

God warned His people again and again, just as parents will warn their children of the consequences of their disobedience, but the wayward children would not listen to their Father.

> **"I warned them again and again, saying, 'Obey me'. But they did not listen or pay attention; instead they followed the stubbornness of their evil hearts. So I brought on them all the curses of the covenant I had commanded them to follow but that they did not keep."** (Jer. 11:7, 8)

Changing the Locks

What was the most severe punishment inflicted by God upon His children? It was their global exile – the loss of their right to live at home in the land God gave to them. As any parent can attest who has been forced into the position of barring a rebellious teen from the family home, the pain felt is immense and the decision not taken lightly. It is a last-ditch move of desperation – of tough love – of saying 'I must draw the line here and cannot stretch it back any further.' The grown child must either conform into some measure of obedience or else leave home.

I will never forget the night they brought my teenage son home, his face so bruised and bloody as to be almost unrecognizable. The doorbell rang insistently in the middle of the night, bringing me into a state of immediate alarm. I had not been sleeping well ever since we gave my rebellious teenager the option of maintaining even a minimal standard of behavior or finding another place to carry out his sinful lifestyle. We warned him over and over again, but he would not listen. He chose to leave. And now here stood strangers at my door, one of them holding my son in his arms. They apparently were his 'friends', who didn't know what else to do with him after members of a Lebanese gang beat him into unconsciousness at a drunken bash. As I laid my son in his familiar bed and covered him with clean sheets, I stroked his hair and wept in anguish at his pain. Despite all the harsh words that had passed between us, I remembered giving birth to him, the softness of his skin, the trials and the joys of his boyhood years, and I grieved the loss of relationship now separating us. A few days later, he was gone again, never sure where he would spend the night or how he would find the means to eat that day. As a mother, did this rip my heart out? Yes. Was it necessary to set a standard for our home? I believe so.

One day, as I was crying out to the Lord and interceding for this son of mine, I felt the Lord showing me that what I feel is, in small part, a measure of how His heart breaks over the continued estrangement between Himself and His people Israel. And yet, just as I still love this firstborn son of mine, despite his behavior, so does the heart of the Father remain unchanging in His love for Israel. He too longs for the day of reconciliation and restoration. Perhaps this day will be soon.

For Us or Against Us?

So what is it? Is God for Israel or against her? At the same time that we know God is for Israel and that He will punish those who come against Israel and Jerusalem, we must also accept the hard fact that the people of Israel are not simply innocent victims. Some people want only to see that God's judgment upon the Jews is justified by their own sin, idolatry and rebellion. Others want only to see God's everlasting love for the Jewish people and the mercy inherent in His character. But God is both the God of justice and of love. The confusion with regards to God's ongoing relationship with Israel stems from a lack of understanding of covenants. The nation of Israel willingly entering into a covenant with God at Mt. Sinai and consented to the terms of this covenant, which are blessings for obedience and curses for disobedience. By sealing the covenant in blood, they ratified it and consented to the consequence of breaking the covenant, which was judgment. Surely the Jewish people have already suffered much, but they have yet to repent of their sins and return with all their hearts to God and His commandments.

The following is an e-mail message I sent out following the collapse of the wedding hall:

May 27th, 2001
Shalom from Jerusalem:

Building Collapse

I'm sure that many of you by now have heard of the tragic accident that occurred Thursday evening in Jerusalem. A relatively new building, in which over seven hundred guests celebrated a wedding that night, collapsed, causing the dance floor and everyone on it to come crashing down three floors into a huge hole in the basement. We live relatively close to where this occurred, and so we heard the sirens of the ambulances and rescue vehicles for several hours. Jerusalem's hospitals were filled to capacity and Hebrew news broadcasts appealed for Israeli citizens to hurry down to donate blood. The information I received is that over two hundred people were injured and twenty-six fatalities. Although because of the degree of rubble, the possibility of finding more bodies existed ; the chance of other survivors is slim. The Rabbinate made special provision for the Orthodox rescue workers to continue their work of searching on Shabbat in the case that a life may be found and saved.

This is a land of such grieving. It was so painful to watch grown men weeping like babies on the news, recalling how the people below stretched their hands up to them screaming for help. Most of them gave the glory to Elohim that they were somehow miraculously of those left standing. Many members of the bride and groom's family were killed or injured. What should have been the happiest day of their lives ended up as the worst non-terrorist, tragedy ever to befall the modern state of Israel.

We cannot help but ask ourselves why? Is it not bad enough that the terrorists continue to set off bombs, killing and injuring the people of Israel. And now this?

To add insult to injury, another car bomb exploded the next day in Hadera. Last night, my daughter Courtney went out with a friend after congregational services in Jerusalem. After being home about an hour, she heard a loud 'boom!' Radek went down to check on the internet, and sure enough, another bomb exploded right where she had been walking only an hour before. Thankfully, no one was injured, even though this area is full of cafes and restaurants.

But God is sovereign; and He is a God of covenant. The parashah (weekly scripture reading) for last Shabbat is called 'B'Chukotai (In My Statutes). Beginning with

Leviticus 26:3, God gives a promise to the people of Israel:

> "If you walk in My statutes, and keep My commandments, and do them; then I will give your rains in their season, and the land shall yield her produce, and the trees of the field shall yield their fruit."

The rains came this year out of season. They came too late to be of any use. The Sea of Galilee is at a dangerously low water level and Israel desperately needs water, but because of the lateness of the rains, they actually caused more destruction to the crops than good. In the previous parashah, B'har, we discussed the laws of sabbatical for the land (Shmittah). This is a Shmittah year for Israel. But many continue to plant, plow, and harvest crops through a kind of religious legal loophole. The Jewish landowners can "sell" their land to a Gentile and therefore continue to work the land during the Shmittah and the fruits and vegetables may then still be considered 'kosher'. But God will not be mocked.

God also promises that IF we keep His commandments (Torah) here in the Land, we will live in the Land in peace, and we will chase our enemies and they will fall before us. That is a tiny word, but it carries with it enormous consequences.

> "If you will not hearken unto Me, and will not do all these commandments; and if ye shall reject My statues, and if your soul abhor Mine ordinances, so that ye will not do all My commandments, but break My covenant; I will also do this unto you; <u>I will appoint terror over you</u>, ...and the soul to languish..." (Lev. 26:14-16)

We must face the probability that God may have appointed

these tragedies and terrors coming upon Israel because of their disobedience to His Torah. I am reminded of the day we had to drive through the 'West Bank' on Shabbat to reach a Messianic congregation in a different city. We got stuck in a traffic jam. Why? Because many Israelis 'shop till they drop' at Palestinian markets on Shabbat in order to get the cheaper prices than in Israel. Well...at least they used to. God commanded the people to keep the Sabbath day holy and not to carry out commerce on this day. Buses do not run and most Jewish businesses are closed; only the Arabs stay open on Shabbat (And Christians?) and some die-hard secular Israelis. Keeping the Sabbath is a special sign of the covenant between God and His people. It is specifically mentioned that for breaking the Sabbath, the people of Israel were exiled from the Land. Also, this week, an idolatrous Bahai centre officially opened in Haifa. Two of the gravest sins - idolatry and profaning the Sabbath - are practiced shamelessly in this country.

Someone has suggested that I write too critically about Israel and that this will cause the love of those who stand with us to wane and grow cold. But I want to help you understand, through our firsthand personal witness, what is actually happening in this country, so that you can pray intelligently and appropriately. As one sister said, *"Love for Israel and the Jews is not a natural thing. It is supernatural and can only be planted in our hearts by God."* I agree. A soulish, emotional kind of 'love' for Israel based on a romantic, unrealistic assessment of the nation will not withstand the end times trials that we will all need to endure. The grace to stand with Israel unto the end with the Lord can only come through His Spirit.

Please don't give up on the nation of Israel, even when we come under such terror and judgment, for God Himself promises never to give up on us, because of His covenant.

God's Plan for Israel

Even when He exiled the people of Israel for their sins into the nations where they were persecuted, tortured, and killed, God did not reject them, nor destroy them completely, nor forget His covenant with Israel.

> **"And yet for all that, when they are in the land of their enemies, I will not reject them, neither will I abhor them, to destroy them utterly, and to break My covenant with them; for I am the Lord their God.**
> **But I will for their sakes, remember the covenant of their ancestors, whom I brought forth out of the land of Egypt in the sight of the nations, that I might be their God; I am the Lord (Anee YHVH)."** (Lev. 26:44, 45)

God warns that He will cause to cease from the cities of Judah and from the streets of Jerusalem the voice of mirth and the voice of gladness, the voice of the bridegroom and the voice of the bride. For the land shall be desolate. (Jer. 7:34)

But the land is beginning to flourish in places. We have in God great promises of restoration for this nation.

> **"And it is the time of Jacob's trouble, but he shall be saved out of it."** (Jer. 30:7)

One day, the sound of joy and gladness, of the bride and the bridegroom will once again be heard in this land. (Jer. 33:11) Yeshua will soon come to take His bride and we will celebrate the true marriage supper of the land - this time with no cave ins!

I also came to see this wedding hall collapse as a prophetic message for people of the nations, even Christians. There existed only one crucial difference between who, in this wedding feast, was saved and who was lost and it was this – where they were standing. The question I believe the Spirit of God is asking His Church is, "Where do you stand with regards to Israel?" Those who take a position of standing with the Palestinians against Israel are standing against God Himself, who is the One that has promised Israel this land. Who was the only one saved out of Jericho? Rahab the prostitute. Was it because of her righteousness? Obviously not! It was only because of the stand she took with regards to Israel. She helped the Israelite spies and only she and her family were saved. In the 25th chapter of Matthew, Yeshua tells us that when He returns, He will separate the sheep and the goats and this is the only criteria of who is saved and who is lost? What kind of practical help and support, what acts of love or kindness did you do or not do for even the least of His brethren? And who did He call His brethren while He walked this earth? The lost sheep of the House of Israel. My heart's cry is for the Christian Church to get out of their narrow viewpoint and scan the wide and wonderful scope of God's word to see His heart for the people and the Land of Israel and for the Church to recognize their covenantal relationship with the Jewish people through the blood of Yeshua Hamashiah, the Jewish Messiah.

False Covenants

There is another reason why Israel is suffering so terribly today from the Palestinian militants and terrorists. It is because of their attempts to enter into a covenant that is not of God. We may look again in the book of Joshua for a Biblical example of false covenant. The people of Gibeon came to Joshua pretending to have come on a long journey from far away, seeking a peace treaty with Israel. Israel fell for their ruse and entered into a treaty with the Gibeonites, but

> "They did not inquire of the Lord first."
> (Josh. 9:14)

This is always our biggest mistake. Acting on wrong information because we neglect to check with the master of the universe first. Before forming opinions about the Israeli-Palestinian conflict, we need to first check out the Word of God! What does God have to say about making a peace treaty with the Palestinians?

Covenants and Boundaries

> **"Make no treaty with them and show them no mercy."** (Deut. 7:2)

God's word is clear about this issue. When Joshua conquered the land,

> **"He left none remaining, but utterly destroyed all that breathed, as the Lord God of Israel had commanded."** (Josh. 10:40)

This is a hard word for us to accept. It was not Israel's aggressive imperialism which caused them to conquer the land and destroy all the inhabitants – all that breathed! – they acted upon the command of the Lord God of Israel. The people of Israel are to make no covenant with the inhabitants of the land; the Palestinians may have a state in whichever place they choose – except one – the Land of Israel. This is the portion of land allotted to Israel. One of the greatest enemies we face today, even in the Church, is 'humanism'. People in the nations, even Christians, misapply the words of Jesus about loving our enemies to construct a humanistic theology of the Middle East conflict, which contradicts the Word of God.

We must come to a confidence in the Word of God that overcomes all our humanistic pity towards what the media shows us about the plight of the Palestinian people. God is the one who has established the borders of the nations.

> **"And He made from one, every nation of mankind to live on all the face of the earth, having determined their appointed times, and the boundaries of their habitation."** (Acts 17:26)

God appointed the boundary for the descendants of Esau:

> **"I have given Esau the hill country of Seir as his own."** (Deut. 2:5)

An Israeli State in Jordan?

God says He will not give even an inch of their land to Israel! Wouldn't it be a ludicrous situation if Israel decided that they desired the hill country of Seir as their land and demanded they be allowed to create an Israeli state in the heart of Mount Seir? Wouldn't it be even more unbelievable for the world to stand with Israel if they began blowing up Arabic men, women, and children in order to 'blackmail' them into giving them this Israeli state that they demand in the middle of the land that God gave to the Arabs?

And yet this is exactly what is happening in reverse! God gave the Arabic people, descended from Esau and Ishmael, great blessings, huge portions of oil rich land. It is only this tiny portion of real estate – 1/10 of 1% of the land mass of the Middle East, that belongs to the people of Israel by divine Covenant, and the world is pressuring Israel to negotiate with these terrorists, and hand over their land to them? What absurdity! Satan, the red dragon, is leading the whole world astray into deception, even the very elect in some Churches. We must stand on the Word of God for our convictions.

Painful Briers and Thorns

God warned us of the painful consequences if we were to disobey Him by leaving the inhabitants of the land amongst us.

> **"But if you do not drive out the inhabitants of the land from before you, then it shall be that those whom you let remain shall be irritants in your eyes and thorns in your sides, and they shall harass you in the land where you dwell."** (Num. 33:55)

Ironically, the Israeli government has joined with the Palestinians to harass and persecute those holding and teaching the view that Israel made a mistake in allowing the Palestinians to remain in the Land. The late Rabbi Kahane, who advocated the expulsion of all Arabs from the land of Israel, was assassinated in New York City several years ago. Just this year, his son and his son's wife were murdered in Israel when Palestinian snipers riddled their car with bullets. All over Israel, graffiti began to appear which read, Kanahe tzadak, which means, Kahane was right (from tzadik – righteous). Israeli police began arresting young radicals wearing T-shirts carrying this slogan. And in the United States, the Kahane offices were raided, their computers and all their equipment seized by the FBI, while acknowledging the unconstitutional nature of the raid and seizure.

People will go to great lengths to keep the truth from the Word of God from being proclaimed.

Spiritual Warfare

The third reason why Israel is experiencing so much persecution is because of the existence of the enemy of our souls – hasatan (the adversary in Hebrew). He hates Israel and especially Jewish Believers, because he knows, even better than we do, God's plans and purposes, which He will work through the nation of Israel. We do not fight against flesh and blood, but against the principalities and powers of darkness that control them. It is not the Muslims, but the spirit of Islam, which seeks to bring the whole world into submission to allah (who is not YHVH God Elohim). If Satan could have destroyed the Jews as he has tried to do so many times in history, there would be no Messiah coming out of the tribe of Judah. If he can destroy Israel and especially Jerusalem he could prevent the Messiah from taking his rightful place on the throne of David. And if he could possibly destroy Israel (which he cannot of course), he would prove the Word of God and therefore God Himself a liar, since God has promised that the nation of Israel would always exist before Him. (Jer.31:36). Contrary to God's word in the next verse (37), satan has convinced a good portion of the Christian Church that God has, indeed, rejected the Jews. I have had a pastor say this to my face and we know that this doctrine exists in replacement theology in some churches. According to this false view, God is through with Israel and the Church is the new Israel. There is one thing, however, that must be reckoned with – the re-emergence of the State of Israel and God's continued workings in this nation. Satan continues to battle against Israel to prove God a liar, and this is why we must endure a fierce spiritual battle against the powers of darkness. Satan is at war with all true Believers, but it is right here, in Jerusalem, where the anti-Christ, the agent of Satan on earth, will attempt to usurp the Kingdom and set Himself up in the temple and proclaim Himself to be God. (2 Thess. 2:4) Satan battles against those churches, which are moving forward and making a difference for the kingdom. But Israel's mere existence enrages the beast!

> "Then the dragon was enraged at the woman and went off to make war against he rest of her offspring – those who obey God's commandments and hold to the testimony of Yeshua." (Rev. 12:17)

Everlasting Covenant

All this is painting a terribly gloomy picture of Israel's future. I'm becoming depressed just writing it! Is Israel under a curse because of her own sins? Is Israel harassed and terrorized by their enemies because they mistakenly let them remain and attempted to enter into a false covenant with them? Is Israel at the top of the page on Satan's hit list? Where is our hope? Where are the great and wonderful promises of the Word of God? They are found in the merciful and faithful character of our God. Even when our own children get themselves in trouble and even when we know their sorrows are their own fault, and even though we usually allow them to learn a lesson from it, doesn't big daddy or mommy eventually step in with 'the big rescue'?

This is where we can trust God to intervene to save Israel with the coming of the Messiah upon the Mount of Olives, just when it looks like all hope is lost. But God is not changeable in His affections. He is a God who establishes, confirms, and operates through covenants with His people. The pathway of hope is through the New Covenant in the Messiah. This New Covenant was promised to the House of Judah and the House of Israel first and then opened up to Gentiles. (Jer. 31:3134; Is. 49:6) The Messiah took upon Himself the curses of the Mosaic covenant. He became a curse for us by hanging on a tree, in order that we could come under the blessings and favor of the Lord our God. Halleluyah!

> "The Messiah has redeemed us from the curse of the law (The curses of the Mosaic covenant), having become a curse for us (for it is written, cursed is everyone who hangs on a tree)." (Gal. 3:13)

This is an everlasting covenant of peace between man and God. I invite you, Jew or Gentile, to enter into this new covenant with our God through faith in His Messiah Yeshua.

> "For a mere moment I have forsaken you, but with great mercies I will gather you. With a little wrath I hid My face from you for a moment; but with everlasting kindness I will have mercy on you, says the Lord, your Redeemer...For this is like the waters of Noah to Me; for as I have sworn that the waters of Noah would no longer cover the earth, so have I sworn that I would not be angry with you, nor rebuke you. For the mountains shall depart and the hills be removed, but my kindness shall not depart from you, nor shall My covenant of peace be removed says the Lord, who has mercy on you." (Is. 54:9, 10)

God's covenant with Abraham through Isaac and Jacob to give their descendants the land of Israel was given by divine promise and cannot be annulled by the Mosaic Covenant.

> "And this I say, that the law, which was four hundred and thirty years later, cannot annul

> the covenant that was confirmed before by God in the Messiah, that is should make the promise of no effect. **For if the inheritance is of the law, it is no longer of promise; but God gave it to Abraham by promise.**" (Gal. 3:17, 18)

God will return His people to this land, as He has returned us, one day to live in peace and security. All painful briers and thorns will be removed.

> **"And there shall no longer be a pricking brier or a painful thorn for the house of Israel from among all who are around them, who despise them. Then they shall know that I am the Lord God."** (Ezek. 28:24)

All enemies will be destroyed when the Lord executes His judgment against them. Under the reign of the Messiah on David's eternal throne, we will live at peace with God and with one another. And all will know that He is the Lord their God (YHVH Elohim).

> **"Then they will dwell in their own land which I gave to My servant Jacob. And they will dwell safely there, build houses, and plant vineyards; yes, they will dwell securely, when I execute judgements on all those around them who despise them. Then they shall know that I am the Lord their God."** (Ezek. 29:25, 26)

When will Israel believe in God and His servant Yeshua? When they see the dead bodies of all those who hated, oppressed and terrorized them.

> **"So the Lord saved Israel that day out of the hand of the Egyptians, and Israel saw the**

> Egyptians dead on the seashore. Thus Israel saw the great work which the Lord had done in Egypt; so the people feared the Lord, and believed the Lord and His servant Moses." (Ex. 14:30, 31)

It happened in the Exodus and it will happen again, perhaps soon, after the battle of God and Magog:

> "For seven months the house of Israel will be burying them, in order to cleanse the land. …So the house of Israel shall know that I am the Lord their God from that day forward." (Ezek. 39:12, 22)

CHAPTER EIGHT

GOD'S PLAN FOR THE NATIONS: DESTRUCTION OF ISRAEL'S ENEMIES

All the earth will know that He is indeed still the Holy One of Israel when He steps His feet upon the Mount of Olives and fights for Israel against all the nations. (Zech.14) Woe to the nations that dare come against Israel, for God's wrath will be upon them. God beckons to the nations to come near enough to Him that they can hear His heart for Israel. Only those close to His heart know how He yearns for Israel. Those who are indifferent, apathetic, or even hostile to Israel show by their attitudes that they have not yet drawn near to God's heart. Israel is the barometer of our relationship with God. Those who support and sympathize with Israel's enemies, whose goal is to annihilate her in these last days, demonstrate their rebellion to God, whether they call themselves the Church or not.

> "Come near, you nations, and listen; pay attention, you peoples!...The Lord is angry with all nations; his wrath is upon all their armies, He will totally destroy them, he will give them over to slaughter, their slain will be thrown out , their dead bodies will send

up a stench; the mountains will be soaked with their blood..." (Is. 34:1-3)

The Spirit of Korach

Israel is destined to a central place, a leadership place amongst the nations of the earth. This is God's plan and will, whether we like it or accept it or not. This is our acceptance of God as God. He chooses whom He chooses. Look at what happened to the rebels who refused to accept God's choice of leadership amongst the Israelites when He led them out of Egypt. Korach and his followers – the elect of the community - came to Moses and Aaron and challenged their leadership.

> **"You have gone too far! The whole community is holy, every one of them, and the Lord is with them. Why then do you set yourselves above the Lord's assembly?"** (Num. 16:3)

In other words, these men were saying to Moses and Aaron, *"Who do you think you are? Why do you make yourself out to be special? We are all holy so why do you try to pretend you are 'chosen'?"* Do you see the parable here? The whole Covenant community of God is holy, but God pre-ordained Israel to be the leader amongst the nations, and Jerusalem the orbit around which all things revolve. Jerusalem is destined to become the place of His eternal government. The gifts and callings of God are irrevocable. The Jewish people who do not accept Yeshua as their Messiah may be enemies of the gospel, but they are still beloved to God on account of the patriarchs. (Rom. 11:2829) We can either choose to accept that this is from God, or to rebel against it. But we need to heed the warning contained in the example of this account. Moses warned the assembly of God to move away from the tents of the rebels and not even touch anything of theirs, lest they be swept away along with Korach and the rebels for their sins. (Num. 16:26) God proved that the appointment of Moses and Aaron's leadership was from Him by swallowing up all the rebels into the earth.

> "They went down alive into the grave, with everything they owned; the earth closed over them, and they perished and were gone from the community." (v. 33)

The Book of Revelations gives a similar warning to the people of God, to separate and remove themselves from all forms of rebellion, represented by Babylon.

> "Come out of her, my people, so that you will not share in her sins..." (Rev. 18:4)

The Word of God warns Believers not to have fellowship with wickedness.

> "Therefore, come out from them and be separate, touch no unclean thing and I will receive you." (2 Cor. 6:17)

God is desperately trying to get through to His people through the mouths of His prophets to move away from the tents of the rebels before His wrath falls upon them, lest they also be swept away into the abyss. The latent anti-Semitism in a segment of the Christian Church is only rearing its ugly head once again, but this time in anti-Zionism. And it uses a ruse of humanistic sympathy and the 'love of Jesus' as a cover. Supporting the Palestinian cause to 'liberate Jerusalem' or any other part of Israel they falsely claim as their own is not helping these people or loving them in any way, shape, or form, but only aiding and abetting their slippery slope to destruction. And unfortunately, these members of the assembly of God may be swept along with their sins.

The Spirit of Jezebel

We need to respect God's appointment of authority, whether that be in our families, our congregations, our governments, or among the nations of the earth. To do any less is rebellion. To attempt to usurp or undermine Godly authority is evidence of a Jezebel spirit that needs to be repented of and cast out of our hearts and homes. We must respect those God has placed in authority over us. This respect must arise out of obedience for God's authority, not based on the character of the person but because of his position. We don't respect our husbands because they are perfect human beings but because God has placed them as head over their wives and to disrespect them is to disrespect God. David, a man after God's own heart, demonstrated this respect for God's election of authority through his dealings with King Saul. Although the King degenerated into such a backslidden state that he persecuted the young David mercilessly without cause, David still chose to spare his life, even when he had opportunity to take it in order to defend his own. Instead, he put his own life at risk by letting King Saul go free in the cave when he came to relieve himself. David refused to harm someone that God had once anointed to leadership. He felt guilty for even cutting the corner of his garment.

Such should be our reaction and attitude towards Israel. For God has said that

> **"Whoever touches her, touches the apple of His eye."** (Zech. 2:8)

Whatever nation that refuses to acknowledge the leadership of Israel amongst the nations, and her centrality to the future government of the Lord, despite her backslidden, degenerate state, will not prosper but will be utterly destroyed.

> **"For the nation or kingdom that will not serve you will perish, it will be utterly ruined."** (Is. 60:12)

This is a fearsome message for the nations of the world. Perhaps the Spirit of God is giving you, the reader, the opportunity to draw near and understand the heart of God towards Israel, in order that you may repent of any apathy, indifference, or rebellion. Perhaps you already knew all of these things and this message is only in your hands to exhort you to tell it to others. We are obligated to warn those being led to the slaughter. If we know and don't warn those who side against Israel and therefore against God, then their blood is on our hands.

Vengeance For Zion's Sake

A Slaughter in Edom

The Word of God has a particular warning for a people called Edom.

> **"My sword has drunk its fill in the heavens; see, it descends in judgment on Edom, the people I have totally destroyed. The sword of the Lord is bathed in blood...For the Lord has a sacrifice in Bozrah, and a great slaughter in Edom..."** (Is. 34:5, 6)

Who is Edom and why does God deliver such a terrible destruction and slaughter upon these particular people? The word Edom in Hebrew is Adom, which means 'red'. It is a name for Esau, brother of Jacob. Esau (Edom) became the father of the Edomites (ancestors of the Arabic people today) and Jacob became the father of the Israelites (ancestors of the Jewish people today).

The continuation of this portion of the prophet Isaiah gives us the reason for the Lord's wrath upon Edom (and all the nations). The answer is – *vengeance for Zion's sake.*

> **"For the Lord has a day of vengeance, a year of retribution, to uphold Zion's cause. Edom's streams will be turned into pitch, her dust into burning sulfur; her land will become blazing pitch it will not be quenched night and day; its smoke will rise forever. From generation to generation it will lie desolate; no one will ever pass through it again."** (Is. 34:8-10)

Why is it that the Edomites cannot see the error of their ways – that they are headed for a collision course with the God of Israel through their violence against their brother Jacob (Israel)? It is because the pride of their hearts has deceived them.

> **"Thus says the Lord God concerning Edom... The pride of your heart has deceived you,... Will I not in that day, even destroy the wise men from Edom, and understanding from the mountains of Esau?...to the end that everyone from the mountains of Esau may be cut off by slaughter. For violence against your brother Jacob, shame shall cover you, and you shall be cut off forever."** (Obad. 1:1, 3, 8-10)

The blood of Jewish men, women and children, even the blood of teenagers staining a Tel Aviv parking lot, cries out to God for vengeance. One day, we will see that vengeance and so that men will say,

> **"Surely He is a God who judges in the earth."**
> (Ps. 58:11)

It is not only the Arabs who will bring upon themselves God's wrath, but all the nations for their treatment of the Jews in the past and for coming against Jerusalem in the future.

> **"Behold, I will make Jerusalem a cup of drunkenness to all the surrounding peoples, when they lay seige against Judah and Jerusalem. And it shall happen in that day that I will make Jerusalem a very heavy stone for all peoples, all who would heave it away will surely be cut in pieces, though all nations of the earth are gathered against it."**
> (Zech. 12:3)

The day of the Lord, which is the day of Yeshua's coming when He will execute judgment upon the nations, is soon coming.

> **"For the day of the Lord upon all the nations is near; as you have done, it shall be done to you; Your reprisal shall return upon your own head."** (Ob. 1:15)

'As you have done, so shall it be done unto you.' Christians in the nations are waking up to the horror of their corporate sins as nations, and repenting before God, in anticipation of His soon coming judgment. Some misguided Christians who failed to help the Jews in the Holocaust, or worse yet, even actively persecuted them, mistakenly believed that since the Jews had 'rejected Jesus', God's wrath was upon them and therefore their mistreatment of the Jews was justified. Many early Church fathers, (including Martin Luther for those who would blame it all on the Catholics), preached venomous words against the Jews.[14] But God has this to say to those people and those nations:

> "I am jealous for Jerusalem and for Zion with great zeal. I am exceedingly angry with the nations at ease; for I was a little angry, and they helped – but with evil intent." (Zech. 2:15)

Yeshua came long ago for the House of Israel as the meek and mild sacrificial lamb who sacrificed His life for the salvation of the world. But when He returns it will be as the Lion of Judah, to execute judgment for Zion's sake against all those who have wronged or mistreated her. When Yeshua read from the scroll of Isaiah in the synagogue, He quoted,

> "The Spirit of the Lord is on me, because he has anointed me to preach good news to the poor. He has sent me to proclaim freedom for the prisoners and recovery of sight for the blind, to release the oppressed, to proclaim the year of the Lord's favor." (Luke 4:18, 19)

Then he rolled up the scroll and sat down, saying to the amazed congregants,

> "Today this scripture is fulfilled in your hearing."

In other words, he read what he would fulfill at this time and then rolled up the scroll to indicate "that's it for now".

He stopped short of quoting the entire scripture. The very next line from Isaiah 61 reads,

> **"And the day of vengeance of our God."**
> (Is. 61:2b)

Why did He not read part 'b' of that line? Why stop in the middle of the verse? Because vengeance was not the purpose of His first coming, but rather salvation. Vengeance is reserved for His Second Coming, which many believe according to the signs of the times, to be very soon. This means that shortly, Yeshua will come with vengeance in his heart against all the enemies of Israel and their allies, but with redemption for Israel.

What will He do to those who say they belong to Him, but mouth a humanistic sympathy for the Palestinian cause? These deceived people need to be warned before they come before Him saying Lord, Lord, and He replies,

> **"Get away from me, I never knew you."**
> (Matt. 7:23)

Those who don't possess a Biblical understanding of the conflict between the people of Israel and the Palestinians in the Middle East today, may have never come into an intimate relationship with the Lord, although they believe they 'know' Him. This is a terrible and tragic mistake. Perhaps the Lord, whose will is that none should perish, is attempting to get someone's attention today?

CHAPTER NINE

GOD'S PLAN FOR THE CHURCH: TO UNIFY WITH ISRAEL

God has a plan. That plan is for the salvation of mankind. This He accomplished on the cross. He also has a plan for Israel and for the Church. All those who stand with Him and with Israel need not fear. The true Church who stands with Israel, like Ruth, has taken protective covering under the blanket of her Kinsman Redeemer. Gentile Christians who love, care for, and help Israel are under the shelter of the wings of the Almighty. Why did Ruth find favor with Boaz, her Redeemer? Because of the kindness she showed to her mother in law. Naomi represents the people of Israel back in the land with all their bitterness, having suffered terrible losses at the hand of the Almighty. The Lord will bless people who show kindness to Israel.

The Bible contains other examples of the Lord blessing and protecting those who help Israel. Rahab is one. When Joshua and his army of Israelite warriors took Jericho, there was only one family saved out of the entire family. It was not because of her righteousness that she was saved, for the scriptures call her a harlot. She and her entire family were saved for one reason alone – because she helped Israel. (Josh. 6:25) Why was Yeshua persuaded to heal the centurion's servant? The elders of the Jews said,

> "'This man deserves to have you do this, because he loves our nation and has built our synagogue.' So Jesus went with them."
> (Luke 7:3-5)

God's word is as true today as it was then – He promises to bless those who bless the children of Israel and curse those who curse them. (Gen. 12:3)

Grabbing Hold of the Jew

It is clear that God's plan is for His people to become joined with Israel in a greater way than we see today.

> "Many nations will be joined with the Lord in that day and will become my people. I will live among you and you will know that the Lord Almighty has sent me to you."
> (Zech. 2:11)

Through the Messiah, He who the Lord Almighty sent to dwell amongst us, the dividing wall between Jew and Gentile has been broken down. Through Yeshua's blood, those who were once far away have been given citizenship in the commonwealth of Israel, membership in the covenants of Promise given to Israel, and an equal position in the family of God. (Eph. 2:11-19)

The prophet Zechariah spoke of a time of restoration in the Land of Israel, at which time non-Jews will grab hold of a Jew in order to find the way to God.

> "This is what the Lord Almighty says: 'In those days ten men from all languages and nations will take firm hold of one Jew by the hem of his robe and say, Let us go with you, because we have heard that God is with you.'" (Zech. 8:23)

How this will come about is not yet ours to see, but we know that God will one day bring Gentile Believers from all the nations to Israel to learn the ways of the Lord through the Torah. In this day, Israel will finally fulfill its missionary destiny as a Light unto the nations.

> "Many peoples will come and say, 'Come, let us go up to the mountain of the Lord, to the house of the God of Jacob. He will teach us His ways, so that we may walk in his paths.' The Torah will go out from Zion, and the word of the Lord from Jerusalem." (Is. 2:3)

God's ultimate plan for the Jewish people and the Church is to form from them the united body of

> "The people of the God of Abraham." (Ps. 47:9)

Yeshua promised that he would bring in other sheep, besides those of Israel and that they would one day be not two separate entities, but one flock under one shepherd.

> "I have other sheep that are not of this sheep pen. I must bring them also. They too will listen to my voice, and there shall be one flock and one shepherd." (John 10:16)

A Note to Non-Jewish Believers

A Peculiar Longing

I realize that many readers of this book are not (as far as one can prove) Jewish by lineage. From many conversations and letters with non-Jewish Believers, I have come to understand that many have a strange, unexplainable yearning in their hearts to also live in the Land of Israel. It is the secret desire of their hearts, which cannot be quenched. As one friend of ours phrased it, 'she'd give up even the favorite family dog' to come to live in Israel. If this applies, you may have no idea why you have this peculiar longing, or even when it started, or how it got inside of you in the first place. All you know is that it is most definitely there. You may have visited the land, or may not, but you feel somehow like Israel is 'home'.

Of course some non-Jewish people do come to live here, but because they cannot obtain citizenship under the law of return, survival is always a struggle.[47] We know of many non-Jews who live here while volunteering for Christian ministries and some who come to visit and end up staying, having children, and living among the Jews in the Land. But in general, Israel is not a country of immigration for non-Jews at this point.

I have recently come across some Biblically based teachings that I believe are inspired from the Holy Spirit regarding the place of non-Jewish Believers within Israel. I hope these ideas will excite and encourage you, as they have for me, and give you a new, fresh perspective on this issue.

---

47 See 'Citizenship under the Law of Return,", Shock Absorption, a Survival Guide for Newcomers to Israel' by Esther Rivkah, p. 8

Restoration of Both Houses of Israel

To make a very long story very short, the nation of Israel was, at one point in their history, divided into two kingdoms or houses. (1 Kin. 11:26, 12:24) The Southern kingdom was the House of Judah, made up of two tribes, Benjamin and Judah. The Northern Kingdom was the House of Israel, made up of the other ten tribes. These ten tribes became known collectively as Ephraimites, after the son of Joseph who received the blessing of the firstborn. The twelve tribes descended from the twelve sons of Jacob (Yaacov), and their names are the twelve gateways to the New Jerusalem. We will have to enter through one of these twelve Israelite gates. (So much for any anti-Semites or anti-Zionists getting into the New Jerusalem, eh?)

Judah was taken to Babylon for 70 years, then later scattered into the nations by Rome in 70 AD. These descendants are what we refer to as 'Jews' – from the tribe of Judah. Yeshua, the Lion of Judah, also descended from this tribe. They wandered among the nations of their exile, but maintained their Jewish identity (to a lesser or greater degree), until God began to re-gather them back to the land in our very generation. The Kingdom of Israel, however, the other ten tribes, were scattered by Assyria in 722 B.C. and became 'lost'.

The Sin of Ephraim

What was the sin of Ephraim, which caused God to be so incensed that He allowed them to be scattered and lost among the nations?

> "The children of Ephraim, being armed and carrying bows, turned back in the day of battle. They did not keep the covenant of

God' They refused to walk in His Torah." (Ps. 78:10)

This was their major sin; they refused to follow the Torah of God.

"I have written for him the great things of My law, But they were considered a strange thing." (Hos. 8:12)

Who is Ephraim?

Clue #1:

Which group of people today, to a large extent refuses to follow the Torah and considers it a 'strange thing', just for the Jews?

This is clue #1. Please keep this in mind as we follow this along further. And so God rejected Ephraim and the tribe of Joseph, father of Ephraim from whom they descend. Instead, He chose Judah.

"Moreover He rejected the tent of Joseph, and did not choose the tribe of Ephraim, but chose the tribe of Judah." (Ps. 78:67)

What happened to Ephraim? Often referred to as the 'lost ten tribes', speculation abounds regarding their whereabouts. The Word of God, however, tells us what happened to them. They were 'sown among the Gentiles' and lost their Israelite identity.

"Ephraim has mixed himself among the peoples;" (Hos. 7:8)

Remember, they (Ephraimites) are not descended from Judah; they are not 'Jews', but they are still most definitely the House of Israel.

> "Israel is swallowed up; now they are among the Gentiles." (Hos. 8:8)

Clue #2:

What other clues do we have about Ephraim?

> "They shall not dwell in the Lords' land, but Ephraim shall return to Egypt, and shall eat unclean things in Assyria." (Hos. 9:3)

Ephraim does not live in the land of Israel; they continue to live among the Gentiles, as Gentiles, eating 'unclean things'. God has declared in His word which of the living creatures are 'clean' and which are 'unclean' (Lev. 11, Deut. 14). Which portion of the People of God eats freely of the things God calls 'unclean'? This is clue #2.

Clue #3:

There is one more characteristic about Ephraim; instead of walking according to God's ways in the Torah, they walk by man-made or human law.

> "Ephraim is oppressed and broken in judgment, Because he willingly walked by human precept." (Hos. 5:11)

Which people group prefer to celebrate man-made festivals and keep human laws instead of the word of God? Perhaps this is not immediately clear. Who celebrates Christmas and Easter (never mentioned in the Bible) rather than the Feasts of the Lord (such as Passover)? Where do we get such human laws such as 'don't drink wine or don't dance, both of which are clearly permitted in the bible? This is clue #3.

I think my point is clear. I don't believe that we have to search for the ten lost tribes in some remote jungle, or on a tiny, undiscovered island. I think that they are right in the midst of the Gentiles in all the nations of the earth. They call themselves Gentiles; they believe in God and Jesus, but they keep many of the ways of the Gentiles rather than the ways of People of God. Because of their paganism, God rejected Ephraim and would no longer call them His people.

> **"Call his name Lo-Ammi (not my people) for you are not My people (Loh Ami), and I will not be your God."** (Hos. 1:8)

God says He will not have mercy upon this rebellious house of Israel.

> **"Call her name Lo-Ruhamah (no mercy), for I will no longer have mercy on the house of Israel but I will utterly take them away; yet I will have mercy on the house of Judah."** (Hos. 1:6, 7)

Clearly, God differentiates here between the two houses or kingdoms: Judah and Israel. All this sounds like bad news and more bad news for Ephraim. But don't despair; there is good news coming.

> **"Yet the number of the children of Israel shall be as the sand of the sea...and it shall come to pass in the place where it was said to them, You are not My people, there it shall be said to them, You are the sons of the living God."** (Hos. 1:10)

God of Mercy

Why does God relent concerning Ephraim? Because our God is a God of mercy; and because He loves His children, even more than we love our own.

> **When Israel was a child, I loved him, and out of Egypt I called my son…I taught Ephraim to walk, taking them by their arms; but they did not know that I healed them. I drew them with gentle cords, with bands of love, and I was to them as those who take the yoke from their neck. I stooped and fed them."**
> (Hos. 11:1-4)

This is a beautiful picture of our Savior, the living bread, who stooped down from His exalted place in heaven to humble Himself in the image of a man. He walked with us on this earth and sacrificed his very life to provide eternal life for whomever would receive him. What a picture of the relentless and all-consuming love of a mother and father! Our God created humanity in His image - male and female He created them. He contains both the male and the female within His nature. Although we generally refer to Him in the masculine, we must not forget his maternal instinct. What parent cannot remember teaching their children to walk, taking them by the arms? Our littlest one just this month began to walk. What a joy! What a triumph! What delight we took in seeing her let go of that one last finger and take her first steps. How our hearts leaped within us! What pride we have now in leading her by her little hand as she walks beside us! How could we ever forget this child or give her up?

> **"'How can I give you up, Ephraim? How can I hand you over, Israel? …My heart**

is changed within me; all my compassion is aroused. I will not carry out my fierce anger...For I am God, and not man – the Holy One among you. They will follow the Lord; he will roar like a lion. When he roars, his children will come trembling from the west...I will settle them in their homes,' declares the Lord."** (Hos. 11:8-11)

One great sorrow for me was the necessity of separating from my eldest son. As much as my desire was for him to make a home for himself with us here in Israel, he decided against making Aliyah and booked a return ticket to Canada, saying that this is a 'crazy place' (which it most definitely can be!). I endured another tearful goodbye to a beloved child. There were times when I would fall into depression or condemnation over us living so far apart. When he is sick, this mother's heart longs to be the one bringing him chicken soup and comfort. This pains my heart so greatly that sometimes it seems beyond my ability to bear. One day, the Lord spoke to me in my grief, and showed me that His heart also yearns for His firstborn, Ephraim.

"Is Ephraim My dear son? Is he a pleasant child? For though I spoke against him, I earnestly remember him still; therefore My heart yearns for him; I will surely have mercy on him, says the Lord." (Jer. 31:20)

The alienation that still exists between G-d and Israel continues to be a source of grief for the Lord. But just as my heart cries out for reconciliation with my firstborn son, and my eyes always strain the landscape for a sign of his return, so too does the Father wait for His prodigal son to come to his senses and return home. The children of Israel will not remain in spiritual estrangement from their God. We have the hope and promise of a wonderful future day of spiritual restoration. This is also a matter of holy covenant. According to a New Covenant God promises to both houses of Israel, He will restore and heal His relationship with His people. Everyone will know the Lord, from the least to the greatest. His Torah will be in their minds and written on their hearts. He will forgive their iniquities and remember their sins no more. (Jer. 31:3134) One day, Judah will come into deeper relationship with God through the knowledge of their Messiah and Ephraim will come into a richer relationship with God through understanding their identity and embracing both the Torah and their brother, Judah.

The Good News

This is the good news – God is a God of restoration. Although Ephraim was scattered among the nations, living as if Gentiles, losing all knowledge of their Israelite identity, yet God promises to once again make them His people and to be their God. He accomplished this through the blood of Yeshua. You "who were once not His people *(Lo-Ammi),*" those upon whom He had not mercy *(Lo-Ruhami)* have now obtained mercy and may now rightfully be called sons and daughters of the living God through the blood of Yeshua Hamashiach (the Messiah). (1 Pet. 2:9; Eph. 2:13,19) When this happens, the two houses, Judah (Yehudah) and Israel (Ephraim) will be gathered together into the re-united commonwealth of Israel.

> **"Then the children of Judah and the children of Israel shall be gathered together…"**
> (Hos. 1:11)

It is upon this unity, that the Lord will command His blessing. Only with this unity of Judah and Ephraim will a united Israel have the force and strength to defeat her enemies. This will happen under one shepherd, one leader, Yeshua the Messiah.

Spiritual Restoration

The Re-Unification of Israel

The prophet Ezekiel foresaw, by the Spirit of God, the re-unification of the two houses. Chapter 37 deals with the Spiritual restoration of Israel. Most people think of this as the time when the Spirit of God will be poured out upon the current people of Israel (Judah) and they will see their Messiah. But Ezekiel tells us of another amazing phenomenon which is about to occur: Judah and Ephraim will become one (echad) in the hand of God.

> "**Thus says the Lord God: 'Surely I will take the stick of Joseph, which is in the hand of Ephraim, and the tribes of Israel, his companions; and I will join them with it, with the stick of Judah, and make them one stick (etz echad) in My hand...'"** (Ezek. 37:19)

This Hebrew word, Echad, is the same word used as in a man shall join to his wife and become one (echad) or

> "**Hear O Israel, יהוה is our God, יהוה is one (echad).**" (Deut. 6:4)

This word can indicate a unity within a plurality.

The Promise of The Land - Not only Judah Re-Gathered

What about, however, the promise of the land of Israel? If this land was promised to the children of Israel, would not this divine sworn oath also apply to the House of Ephraim as well as the House of Judah?

> "Surely I will take the children of Israel from among the nations, wherever they have gone, and will gather them from every side and bring them into their own land..." (Ezek. 37:21)

We usually think of the re-gathering of the exiles as only referring to the Jews, but these scriptures make clear that the re-gathering will be for ALL of Israel. Isn't it ironic that Ephraim may actually be assisting Judah to make Aliyah, (Exobus, Christians for Israel, etc.) when they too will one day be gathered to the Land!

But how could this tiny land of Israel (getting smaller every time our leaders give another piece of it away!) ever have enough room to contain all these people? This is a question that many people ask and it is a puzzling one. To this, I offer a possible answer. First of all, the borders promised to Israel are much larger than the borders of the nation of Israel today. Secondly, 2/3 of the people of the land will be cut off in the war and judgment that is coming. (Zech. 13:8) Thirdly, it is not all the Church that wants to embrace the same Torah as Israel and live by 'one standard and one law' (Num. 15:15) with Judah. Only a small remnant of God-Seekers is being called out to join with Judah in the Land. Also, we know that the day will come when so many will want to make aliyah that they will be crying out that there is not enough room, and wanting more space here in Israel. (And we thought we had a problem with population density now!)

> "For your waste and desolate places, and the land of your destruction, will even now be too small for the inhabitants; And those who swallowed you up will be far away. The children you will have, after you have lost

the others, will say again in your ears, 'the place is too small for me; give me a place where I may dwell.'" (Is. 49:19, 20)

Those God sowed among the Gentiles will return to God through the Messiah, Yeshua, but a remnant will also return to the Land.

> "I will whistle for them and gather them, for I will redeem them...I will sow them among the nations, and they shall remember Me in far countries; they shall live, together with their children and they shall return... Until no more room is found for them." (Zech. 10:8-10)

Do you long for your home in Israel, my precious brother and sisters from the House of Israel? Listen for the whistle of God.

Judah's Sins

If I have made it seem as if the House of Israel (Ephraim) was so bad that God rejected them, but Judah has been the 'good kid' in the family, then I've given the wrong impression. In Israel today, much of the nation, Judah, defiles itself with every sin, indulging in all manner of idolatry and transgression. Stores are full of New Age books and symbols, sorcery, and occultism. Instead of celebrating Purim, the kids dress up as witches and vampires and glorify the kingdom of darkness, mimicking the Gentile's love of Halloween. But one day, when Israel is re-united, the land will be cleansed of all this filth. This will only happen when Yeshua returns to take up His throne and to save us.

> "And I will make them one nation in the land, on the mountains of Israel; and one king shall be king over them all; they shall no longer be two nations, nor shall they ever be divided into two kingdoms again. They shall not defile themselves anymore with their idols, nor with their detestable things, nor with any of their transgressions; but I will deliver them from all their dwelling places in which they have sinned, and will cleanse them. Then they shall be my people and I will be their God." (Ezek. 37:19-23)

How we long for that day.

Already we see this re-unification happening. The children of Ephraim are waking up to their true identity. They are forsaking paganism, adopting the Torah, celebrating the Feasts of the Lord, eating only Biblically 'clean foods', standing with their Jewish brothers and sisters around the world and especially in the Land of Israel, and praying and interceding for the welfare of the nation of Israel. But one day, this unity will take place in an even greater way, when we all live together here in the Land under the reign of Moshiach ben David, (Messiah, Son of David).

> "David My servant shall be king over them, and they shall all have one shepherd; they shall also walk in My judgments and observe My statutes and do them. Then they shall dwell in the land that I have given to Jacob My servant, where your fathers dwelt; and they shall dwell there, they, their children, and their children's children, forever; and My servant David shall be their prince forever." (Ezek. 37:24, 25)

Halleluyah. Selah.

Spiritual Opposition

God is beginning to fulfill His word to pour out His spirit upon His people all over the world. Messianic Judaism – Jews who believe that the Messiah has come as Yeshua of Nazareth – is growing so rapidly, both within and outside Israel, that it is now perceived by the Jewish religious leaders as Judaism's most serious threat. Well - funded Orthodox Jewish organizations have embarked upon an all out campaign to counteract the biblical claims made by Messianic Believers about knowing the Messiah of Israel. In Israel at the present time, the Messianic Action committee reports believers' homes being trashed and firebombed. Messianic bookstores regularly receive bomb threats, and individual believers' lives have been threatened. One evening, we decided to visit a Messianic bookstore in Tel Aviv. As we prepared to leave, a staff member warned us that an anti-missionary group had set up their 'video-taping' station in front of the store. Indeed, a young man dressed in the traditional black hat and coat and the long earlocks, was videotaping everyone who entered or exited the store. This is just another intimidation tactic, designed to discourage Israelis from obtaining Messianic material. Still, the Lord is greater than any opposition. He is our shield and our salvation. What is a mortal man in comparison to our mighty God?

Zeal for the Lord

One Messianic congregation in Be'ersheva was attacked by Ultra- Orthodox Jews after receiving false information that these 'Christians' were preparing to baptize hundreds of Jewish children, thereby 'stealing their souls'. Several zealots forced their way into the building, hunting for the baptismal tank, even standing right on top of it while shouting to each other, "You liars! There is no such thing in this place!" (The Lord must have an incredible sense of humor). Some, in their misguided zeal, attempted to forcibly remove the children from their parents, even a nursing child from its mother's breast. Although they believed they were acting out of zeal for the Lord, the children of this congregation especially, suffered much trauma through this attack, and continue to have recurring nightmares. One zealous Yeshiva student was quoted as saying, 'I am just waiting for the rabbi's permission to kill them.' Why? The Torah says,

> "If your very own brother, or your son, or daughter, or the wife you love, or your closest friend secretly entices you, saying 'Let us go and worship other gods' (gods that neither you nor your fathers have known, god of the peoples around you, whether near or far, from one end of the land to the other), do not yield to him or listen to him. Show him no pity. Do not spare him or shield him. You must certainly put him to death. Your hand must be the first in putting him to death, and then the hands of all the people. Stone him to death, because he tried to turn you away from the Lord your God, who brought you out of Egypt, out of the land of slavery. Then all Israel will hear and be afraid, and no one among you will do such an evil thing again."
> (Deut. 13:6-11)

If we put ourselves for a moment 'in their shoes', we may see how their violent attempts to prevent Messianic Jews from sharing their faith in Yeshua, is in their eyes completely justified, and even righteous. After all, didn't Pinchas the zealot, turn the anger of the Lord away from the Israelites by driving a spear through both Zimri, the Israelite, and Cozbi, the Midianite, who committed sexual immorality right in the Israelite camp? Because Pinchas was zealous for the honor of his God and made atonement for the Israelites with the pair's blood, he and his descendants were given a covenant of a lasting priesthood. (Num. 25) God does not take idolatry lightly, nor should we. That is why it is imperative that we do all we can to restore the knowledge of the true identity of the Messiah as a Hebrew, a Jew, the son of the God of Israel. He is not 'some foreign god that our forefathers have not known, and certainly not the exclusive god of the goyim around us, but Immanu-El (God with us).

It is possible that the numbers of Haredi (extremists religious Jews) who believe, that Yeshua is the Messiah of Israel are much higher than we could even suspect. We have received unconfirmed reports that they exist, but like Esther, are remaining quiet in obedience to the Holy Spirit until their time has come. Jews who receive Jesus as their savior, and 'convert' to Gentile Christianity, abandoning the laws and commandments of their God, decorating Christmas trees and eating bacon and eggs with the church crowd are still considered a tragic case by the Jewish community. They do not, however, represent as powerful a 'threat' as the testimony of a Jew who receives Yeshua as Messiah and thus turns back to a lifestyle of Torah observance with a new heart and new spirit as promised:

> **"I will give you a new heart and put a new spirit in you; I will remove from you your heart of stone and give you a heart of flesh. And I will put my Spirit in you and move you to follow my decrees and be careful to keep my laws."** (Ezek. 36:26, 27)

Stand Firm

As a consequence of this spiritual awakening, spiritual opposition can be expected to increase. As they hated Him, we can expect them to hate us.

> **"All men will hate you because of me, but he who stands firm to the end will be saved."** (Mark 13:13)

Yeshua warned us there would come a day when those who kill His followers will think they are doing God a favor.

> **"In fact, a time is coming when anyone who kills you will think he is offering a service to God."** (John 16:2)

We must determine to stand firm and not to fear them.

> **"I tell you, my friends, do not be afraid of those who kill the body and after that can do no more. But I will show you whom you should fear. Fear him who, after the killing of the body, has power to throw you into hell. Yes, I tell you, fear Him."** (Luke 12:4, 5)

We must remember the response of Yeshua and His early followers to the Jewish zealots who persecuted them,

> **"Father, forgive them, for they don't know what they are doing…Don't hold these sins against them."** (Luke 23:34)

Although they are enemies of the gospel, they are still beloved of God,

> "As far as the gospel is concerned, they are enemies on your account; but as far as election is concerned, they are loved on account of the patriarchs, for God's gifts and his call are irrevocable." (Rom. 11:28, 29)

Laboring in the Harvest Fields

All this persecution and opposition is only serving to further God's purposes as the plight of Messianic Jews is publicized in the Israeli media. More and more Israelis are becoming aware of, and even curious about the claims of Messianic believers to know the Messiah of Israel. When Yeshua saw the multitudes in Israel, He was moved with compassion for them, because they were weary and scattered, like sheep having no shepherd. (Matt. 9:36) So, too, are the masses in Israel weary and lost today, having little faith in either their government or in God as they see Him in the religious community of faith. But Yeshua told his disciples a truth that is still applicable today,

> "The harvest truly is plentiful, but the laborers are few. Therefore pray the Lord of the harvest to send out laborers into His harvest." (Matt. 9:37, 38)

The other day, I met Liat's former baby-sitter on the bus, Ella - a dear, older Russian woman. She looked so weary of life. When I asked how she was feeling, she answered with a shrug,

"Kacha, kacha", which is a phrase in Hebrew meaning, "like this and like that…" or roughly, 'O.K….sort of'.

It was the situation in the country that was getting her down. She quit her present job because her Israeli employer screamed at her like a 'smartut' (an old dish-rag). I gave her some encouragement and job suggestions, and she seemed much brighter when we got off the bus together. She waved goodbye, saying, *"I think God sent you to me."*

Later that day, on our way to the congregational service, I happened to see Ella again. The Holy Spirit convicted me that I need to invite her to our services. I had shared with her that we are Messianic Jewish Believers, but never gotten farther than this point. The next day, I called and invited her to our 'kehilla' (congregation) and she was delighted to receive our invitation. We are praying that the Spirit of God will touch Ella's heart and that she will receive a new life and new hope both now and eternally through Yeshua Hamashiach.

The Lord presents us with many opportunities to share Yeshua in our day to day relationships with the people of Israel. Some oppose the gospel, but there are many others who, like Ella, are just waiting to be invited to the harvest feast. May we serve the Lord here 'with all humility and even with tears and with trials that come upon us through those who oppose the gospel of Yeshua Hamashiach.' May the gospel come forth through us 'in power and in the Holy Spirit and with full conviction' that we may reap in the Lord's harvest fields here in the Land and in the nations.

ONLY IN ISRAEL...

The Bloopers

On our first day in the Land, someone stood up at the Be'ad Chaim[48] (pro-life) conference and said that this is a place where just waking up in the morning is an adventure! At that time, I didn't know what he was talking about, but now I think I have a better idea. I would like to share with you some of these adventures, which I entitle, 'Only in Israel'. I didn't want this book to be primarily about theology (as much as I love the Word of God); but rather a collection of stories shared from my heart about my life's journey. I hope that by some crazy miracle, these re-collections would be a blessing and encouragement and even an inspiration to you. So here goes – the bloopers.

The following, in true Israeli style, is going to be an assorted, disorganized, uncensored selection of correspondence from Israel to friends and family outside the Land, and to people and organizations within Israel. I hope that collectively, despite its lack of structure, you will be able to put together a more realistic picture of daily life in Israel, especially for a Messianic Jewish Believer, a wife and a mother, immigrating to this strange and wonderful land called Eretz Yisrael (The Land of Israel). Brace yourself! You're about to hear the good, the bad, and the ugly about 'The Holy Land'.

---

48 Be'ad Chaim Association, P.O. Box 7974, Jerusalem 91078, Israel, www.beadchaim.org

THE JERUSALEM SYNDROME

Dear David:

I re-read your message today and thanks - I needed that - joy comes in the morning. Today was a real howdy-do howler day. Have any of those? But I am seeing a glimmer of light and hope. Or is it the coffee? Oh please forgive the unspiritual tone of this letter. I think it's called Jerusalem syndrome. Heaven forbid. But really, many people completely lose it in this city. I had such a strange encounter in the post office yesterday. Went with an American friend to mail some newsletters and this woman was staring at me with weird, buggy eyes. So I tried to avoid her, but sure enough, she came over and asked where I am from. *"Canada"*, I replied. She had a strange smile on her face. *"My friend is from the States"*, I added, hoping to deflect her attention to my friend (thanks, she says). This woman asks me if I am religious. *"Well,... I have faith in God..."* I lamely replied. She leaned right into my ear and whispered, *"I am a Messianic Jew!"* *"Oh, great"*, I say, *"We are Believers, too"* (loud enough for the whole post office to hear). She goes on to tell me that they are keeping her in a mental institution and persecuting her because she is a Believer. *"The Holy Spirit told me you are a Believer"*, she said. *"And I know that you know who I am, because I saw you looking at me."* "She pauses" for effect – *"I am the Lord's wife!"*

"Oh!?" She walks out, very happy that I recognized that she is the Lords' wife. Oh dear. The former editor of the _____ unfortunately also had to be institutionalized. Since you don't know his or her name, I think I am safely not telling tales out of school. But please pray for my mental state – I'm not kidding. It happens here. Today, at my wits end with Liat and covered in baby vomit, I shouted, *"I'm losing my mind!!!!!!!!!!!!!!"* And then screamed, just for effect - in case anyone cared. That brought hubby out of his

pajamas. But really I am convicted that I have to stop talking this way and confess a sound mind and all the other good things that we can claim in our new life in Yeshua.

Well, I really sounded off, didn't I? Now I understand why sometimes, perfect strangers confess intimate details of their life to me over e-mail. Everyone needs someone to talk to, eh? (see, I'm still part Canadian).

Shalom and God bless you out of Zion.
Love Hannah

Lakhatz Means Frustration

I am really struggling with what is called in Hebrew, "lakhatz", which is roughly translated into English as 'frustration' or pressure. Not knowing otherwise how to write the guttural sound for which we have no English equivalent, I've written it as 'kh', but it's pronounced as if you're trying to get a chicken bone out of your throat. Now I know that everyone suffers from 'lakhatz' at some point or another, but it is a serious matter when this is the cause for Believers to leave the country. Although we are well aware of the murderous terrorist acts all over our country, believe it or not, it is the daily frustration of living in this confusing country that is driving people out. Today, after spending a few hours on the phone getting absolutely nowhere, I just broke down in tears - not longing for the leeks and garlic of my Egypt (Canada), but just for a friendly voice on the phone giving the name of the organization and asking if they may be of service, just some semblance of efficiency, some minute trace of common courtesy. How I miss businesses that are open during regular office hours instead of whenever they willy nilly feel like it, and government departments that can transfer a file in a few days, instead of a few months, maybe...

But, as my Israeli brother in law always says, *'This is Israel'*. That phrase is starting to really bug me. ☺

I spoke to a woman whose children are at my son, Shmuel's school in the Old City. Originally from Khazakstan, she married a Jewish man and lived in Tzfat for several years, also in the Haredi[49] community, studying for conversion. She has since become a Believer in Yeshua, but is also now a single mother with her children in Jerusalem. Although she has lived here for over eleven years, she is beginning to question whether or not to remain in Israel.

"Why?" I asked.

Is it because of fear for her children's safety, financial concerns, or God calling her elsewhere? No, it is because of the continual and relentless assault of daily frustration. As she confirmed, so many of the people seem a touch 'meshugah' (off-balance is a nice way of putting it).

Although I had previously 'blamed the devil' for all the *lakhatz* and confusion here in the Land of Israel, I recently have come to see that this may still be a part of the curse of the Mosaic Covenant. The Word warns that if the people do not keep the covenant of Torah,

> **"The Lord will strike you with madness and blindness and confusion of heart."**
> (Deut. 28:28)

Certainly the majority of the people of Israel are not living in accordance with the Torah, for which God promises His great blessings. Even the religious abide more by the Talmud and tradition than the Torah. I think we can well apply the ancient words of the Psalmist to the situation in the Land today:

---

49   Haredi are ultra-Orthodox Jews.

> "You have shown Your people hard things;
> You have made them drink the wine of
> confusion." (Ps. 60:3)

But this surely cannot explain it all. Yesterday, a young Jewish Believer from East Germany came over and broke down in tears of frustration. These were her general words, *"I can't take living where I am any more. There are prostitutes and drug dealers coming and going at all hours of the day or night and discos blaring music even throughout shabbat. The pipes have burst and I'm freezing, but I can't afford any other place to live. I'm a licensed social worker in my country but can't find any work here in Israel. I am cleaning houses, but even this is not enough. I have no family here and am tired of being all alone. If I had stayed in my country, I probably would have been married with several children by now. But here I am with nothing and no one and I wonder what I am doing here?"*

Miriam had, before becoming a follower in Yeshua, been part of the Haredi community - the ultra-orthodox whose women shave their hair and cover their heads with wigs and scrupulously follow all the laws of Rabbinical Judaism. Although she was persecuted and driven out of their community when she was baptized (immersed in the mikvah[50]), she confesses that the Orthodox Community well takes care of its own. Because of the heavy funding they receive from outside the Land, and the commandments in Torah to care for the poor and needy, the entire community cares for those in difficult situations. No one is left hungry or to sleep on the streets. Even marriages can be arranged. In contrast, the Messianic Community in Israel is just struggling to keep its head above water. Even much of the Christian funding goes to Orthodox sources rather than seeking out

---

50 Mikvah – ritual water immersion, practiced by Yeshua and John the Baptist (Yochanan the Immerser).

the Believing Remnant in the Land. I hope this will change, that we will, as a body, become better equipped to help our own.

After this very 'heavy' e-mail, I think we all need a good laugh, so I'm going to close with a 'conversation' between Saddam and Yitzchak that certainly brought a smile to my face. Thanks Russ, I needed that.

Saddam Hussein was sitting in his office wondering who to invade next when his telephone rang.

"*Hallo! Mr. Hussein,*" a heavily accented voice said.

"*This is Yitzhak down in Tel Aviv, Israel. I am ringing to inform you that we are officially declaring war on you!*"

"*Well, Yitzhak,*" Saddam replied, "*This is important news! Tell me, how big is your army?*"

"*At this moment in time,*" said Yitzhak after a moment's calculation, "*there is me, my cousin Saul, my next-door neighbor Shlomo, and the entire pinnochle team from the deli -- that makes eight!*"

Saddam sighed. "*I must tell you, Yitzhak, that I have one million men in my army waiting to move on my command.*"

"*Oy vey!*" said Yitzhak, "*I'll have to ring you back!*"

Sure enough, the next day Yitzhak rang back.

"*Right, Mr. Hussein, the war is still on! We have managed to acquire some equipment!*"

"*And what equipment would that be, Yitzhak?*" Saddam asked.

"*Well, we have two combine harvesters, a bulldozer and Goldberg's tractor from the kibbutz.*"

Once more Saddam sighed. "*I must tell you, Yitzhak, that I have 16 thousand tanks, 14 thousand armored personnel carriers, and my army has increased to one and a half million since we last spoke.*"

"*Really?!*" said Yitzhak, "*I'll have to ring you back!*"

Sure enough, Yitzhak rang again the next day.

"Right, Mr. Hussein, the war is still on! We have managed to get ourselves airborne! We've modified Moshe's ultralight with a couple of rifles in the cockpit and the bridge team has joined us as well!"

Saddam was silent for a minute, then sighed.

"I must tell you Yitzhak that I have 10 thousand bombers, 20 thousand MIG-19 attack planes, my military complex is surrounded by laser-guided surface-to-air missile sites, and since we last spoke, my army has increased to two million."

"Oy gevalt!" said Yitzhak, "I'll have to ring you back."

Sure enough, Yitzhak called again the next day.

"Right, Mr Hussein, I am sorry to tell you that we have had to call off the war."

"I'm sorry to hear that," said Saddam. "Why the sudden change of heart?"

"Well," said Yitzhak, "We've all had a chat, and there's no way we can feed two million prisoners."

We All Need a Laugh

Two Rabbis at the Final Vow of Nuns

At a Mass at which some young ladies were to take their final vows to become nuns, the Bishop presiding noticed two Rabbis enter the church just before the service began. They sat on the right side of the center aisle. The Bishop wondered why they had come, but he didn't have time to inquire before the Mass began. When it came time for the announcements, the Bishop's curiosity got the better of him. He welcomed the two Rabbis and asked why they had chosen to be present at this occasion where the young ladies were to become the "Brides of Christ."

The elder of the Rabbis slowly rose to his feet and explained,

"Family of the Groom."

Kids Say the Funniest Things

Yesterday, we enjoyed a real Brazilian fiesta with Sarah and Mordechai. I decided to dress up in a black dress and a beautiful silk scarf that my wonderful husband bought for my birthday. Timothy (Shmuel in Hebrew), my seven year old son, took a long look at me and said, *"Hey Mom, you know, you look between twenty and thirty-nine years old."* Pretty wide range, I'd say!

Noticing that he received some laughs in response to this comment, he ventured further, *"Actually, in that dress no one can tell..."* *"Can tell what, son?"* I asked

In apparent innocence, he replied, *"No one can tell that you're old!"* ☺

Phone Frustration

I am really struggling with frustration. This is how it works here: I called the number listed in the book for the office. A message comes on saying the number has been changed. You must add a 6 in front of the number and dial again. So I called this new number and a message comes on again, saying this number has been changed to a new number. So I called this new number, and... we go through the same ordeal again. I *finally* got through to a human voice who hollered loudly, *"KEN!!"* (Yes)

That's it? What happened to... *"Shalom, this is the office of _____, may I help you?"*?

We Canadians are so used to politeness and relative efficiency in service. So I asked him about the matter I called about and he said they are closed and will not be open until Monday (This is Thursday). O.K. I just confirm the address that is in the book. No, no, he says, that's not the correct address, the right address is _____. (Mind you, this guy doesn't speak a word of English, so thank God I can speak *any Hebrew at all*.) Then he asked me,

"Is it just yourself you are applying for?

"No," I answer, *"for my whole family."*
"Oh", he says, *"That's a whole different story"*
Now that means we have to go to an entirely different address, so we go through the whole process of the address again, I'm trying to make out his Hebrew accurately to get the address and directions in Tel Aviv. No, he doesn't know the name of the office building, and no, he doesn't know their phone number, but they will be open Sunday[51]. I have a sinking feeling in my gut that we will pay the quadrillion sheckels to take the bus down to Tel Aviv, the kadruple zillion sheckels for a cab to find this place, get up at 5 in the morning to get there before it closes, and then find the address doesn't exist or it's not the right office, or they don't even know what we're talking about. It's probably the S.P.C.A or shelter for unwanted new immigrants or something. Halleluyah! Just about going nuts. I need some peace. O.K. peace, I'm ready for ya. You can come anytime now....I'm waiting....still waiting... O.K. I'm going to the beach.

Lying

If there's one thing you can count on in Israel, it's that people are probably not telling you the truth. This is a hard thing for us nice Canadians to accept – that people will just out and out lie. Especially since we live in Israel and it was to Israel that God gave the Ten Commandments and one of them says, 'Thou shalt not lie', and Israel said, "Whatever you have said, we will do..." Of course not everyone in Israel is a liar, but some most definitely lie. Maybe it goes way back to Abraham, Isaac, and Jacob our forefathers, all of whom were liars and deceivers. Maybe this unrepentant sin has brought a curse upon this nation. But for whatever reason, it's here and has to be dealt with at some time or other. Take for example the time Shelley's kids didn't come

---

51 Sunday is called Yom Rishon, the first day of the week and is a normal business working day.

home from school on the monit (taxi). My friend, Shelley, from Ariel, had arranged a taxi service to bring her children home from kindergarten every afternoon. We were sitting in her living room, enjoying a cup of coffee and a nice chat, when all of a sudden, Shelley jumped up, looking anxious. She realized that it was awfully late, and her little ones were not yet home from school. She phoned the driver of the taxi on his cell phone and he assured her that the children were sitting right beside him, and that they would be home shortly. Immediately after she hung up, she received a call from the gan (kindergarten). The ganenet (kindergarten teacher) was asking Shelley why her children had not yet been picked up from gan?

"*But I just received a call from the driver.*", Shelley exclaimed. "*He just told me the children are with him!*"

"*They most definitely are not*", replied the ganenet. "*They're sitting here waiting to be picked up.*"

Shelley, extremely upset, called back the driver, saying, "*I just received a call from the gan and my children are not picked up yet, so they are <u>not</u> with you, are they!*"

"*Oh, I guess they are not*", he says as a matter of fact. It would be one thing if they were actually sorry for being caught in a bold faced lie, but usually they're indignant, like 'so what!'. Apparently, the driver had a flat tire, and not wanting to worry the parents, said the children were already with him and would be home shortly. Chutzpah,[52] eh? I found a lovely scripture promise to give us hope and patience – (savlanut) Liars beware!

> **"The remnant of Israel shall do no unrighteousness and speak no lies, nor shall a deceitful tongue be found in their mouth; for they shall feed their flocks and lie down, and no one shall make them afraid."** (Zeph. 3:13)

---

52 chutzpah is roughly translated as 'what nerve' or 'gall!"

Shopping for Prunes in Israel

I went to buy prunes to make *hamentashen*, the traditional triangular cookies for Purim (called *oznei haman* in Hebrew, meaning ears of Haman) , but it was a struggle. First, I didn't know how to say prune in Hebrew. I was trying to tell them that I wanted the stuff to make my own hamentashen, but they kept showing me all the yucky ones they had already made, which are hard as rocks and not at all like mama used to make in Canada. Finally, we got to the prunes, and I learned the Hebrew word. (Should have looked it up in the dictionary before I went). They told me prunes cost 33 sheckels a kilo and so I get 1/2 a kilo of these dried up looking prunes sealed in a plastic bag. I go into another store, and notice that he has beautiful, plump, prunes in bulk. So I ask how much and he says 26 sheckels a kilo. Already I know I've been ripped off. I check how much are the little '*shalach munos*' candy boxes for the kids. I shouldn't have asked. They're only 7.50 and guess how much I paid? Right, 11 sheckels. So I go back to the first store and ask if I can return the prunes at least. They never give you your money back here, but they did mark my name down for a credit towards my next purchase. Oh well. At least I got my prunes.

Customer Service in Israel

Shopping for groceries at the co-op yesterday was a real treat as well. I went in for just a few items, but as usual, filled the grocery cart. We got off to a shaky start. I needed five sheckels for the cart and only had a 50 sheckel bill, so I asked for change at customer service. She wouldn't give me change, but asked me to leave my teudat zehut (identity card). I thought, 'Now this is getting ridiculous! I know you need a teudat zehut to do just about anything in Israel, but - for a grocery cart - you've got to be kidding me!' My husband, Radek, was just about hit the roof! After everything we went through to get that card, he was not about to let it out of our possession, especially not to get a grocery cart. We have a little portable cart on wheels that will hold a few bags, so we took that in, but security stopped us, saying, *"Asoor, asoor!" (Not allowed!")* I thought Radek was really going to lose it right there and then. Thankfully, the customer service (if you can call it that) clerk had mercy on us and decided to buck the system and give me change after all to get a grocery cart so I can collect my groceries.

O.K. You think that's the end of it. Right? Wrong! We get to the checkout, and of course it was more than we expected to spend, so I didn't have enough cash on me. Neither was there enough to cover the full amount of 535 sheckels in the account. So I gave the cashier 200 sheckels in cash and wrote a cheque for 400, expecting her to give me the change in sheckels. Oh no, this would be too easy for Israel. The cashier had already punched in 200 cash, so the cheque was too much and she could not (for some vague reason) adjust her register, so they called over the manager, and they're hollering back and forth what to do about this dilemma. Meanwhile, the lineup behind us is getting longer and longer and the people more and more disgruntled. Finally, the manager decided what to do. (No, I didn't have another cheque, and no, I could not change the amount on the cheque and initial the changes. They don't accept that in Israel). The manager voided the whole transaction and started all over again - ringing in every single item by the number codes. Everyone had to move to the next cashier. Groans....Oy, vey...O.K., they accept it. Mah La-asot? (What can you do?) *"No! No!"*, the cashier screams, after they've moved to the next cashier. *"Cashier number seven!"*. So they all moved again. (Probably thinking, 'just another day in Israel') Can you imagine how long it took for her to ring in 535 sheckels worth of groceries again by number code?

I was so exhausted when I got home. I think I might turn into one of those neurotic people that never leave their apartments. I'll never complain about customer service in Canada again.

More Shopping Trivia

October 26th, 2000

A synagogue in a grocery store?

Even in these troubled times, we have to find something to laugh about. Israel is definitely a unique country. My 7 year old son, Shmuel, came grocery shopping with me the other day. In Israel, one has three choices for shopping: the makolet, which is a close, convenient, small, and friendly neighborhood food market, like a 7/11. Nice, but very expensive and limited selection. Or you can brave the shook - definitely an exotic Middle Eastern market experience. Be prepared for a lot of shouting, pushing and shoving - sometimes you wonder if the people have totally lost their marbles or are just getting excited. Some of the aisle ways are so crowded you can barely squeeze in or out - definitely a tough place to come shopping with little children - but the prices are good and the fruits and vegetables fresh and delicious. Finally, there is the 'Super' - this is a rough duplicate of a North American grocery store. But they are very crowded, and whoever designed them built the aisles too narrow for the large and awkward grocery carts to pass one another. The inevitable result is a massive grocery cart traffic jam, to which many people seem oblivious, just pushing people out of the way with their carts. Shmuel was my navigator this time- we thought maybe people would feel sorry for a kid and let him through. My silent prayer went up to heaven, *"Oh please give me Safeway!"* Shmuel told me that there is a shule (synagogue) in the grocery store. Of course, I thought he was joking, but he was very serious. *"This, I will not believe until I see it with my very own eyes"*, I thought. Sure enough, there was the shule (actually more of a prayer room with siddurs (prayer books) available for the public. Maybe the people go to the shule to pray that they will have enough sheckels to pay for their groceries – or that they get out alive?

Only in Israel....

Oh, the Drawers are Extra – Furniture shopping in Israel

Radek and I also went looking for a desk. Actually Radek went on his own first (big mistake) and came back with two huge boxes. Inside were probably one hundred pieces of wood of various sizes and shapes, a bag with about a thousand screws (at least it looked like that many), and glue.... Oh yes, included were pages and pages of instructions with diagrams and Hebrew lettering. None of the pieces of wood to assemble were numbered or marked in any way to correspond with the diagram. But Radek was determined! After several hours, he decided that the manufacturer drilled the holes in the wrong places and several pieces were backwards. Did the store have anyone available to put the unit together? No. But they gave us the number of someone - Momo. We called Momo, but it wasn't Momo, it was someone else who was just a delivery boy, but he felt sure if we called the store, they would give us the number of Momo who might know someone who might be able to put it together....right! So Radek unscrewed all the pieces he had screwed together, tried to fit all the pieces back together in the box and returned it to the store. The only reason they took it back is because it was already closing hours, so they just gave him a credit slip. Israel has not discovered the concept of 'satisfaction or your money refunded'. They only give credit to exchange. So we went back to the store together today (better plan) and picked out a more simple desk - just 2 flat pieces of wood joined by a metal rod. One piece cost 299 sheckels and the other, 150. What I found outrageous, however, was the fact that a sign was tacked onto the 2 small plastic drawers underneath reading 269. It couldn't possibly mean that the drawers cost an additional 269 sheckels, could it? It must be a code number. We finally found someone to help us, which was a bit of a task in this store that was an approximate Middle Eastern imitation of a Canadian Tire or Home hardware store - except with aisles so full of cartons and large boxes and merchandise that you couldn't push your cart through! I asked the clerk and, sure enough, the drawers to the desk are not included and cost an additional price which is almost as much as the desk itself.

Only in Israel....

Jews Have Black Hearts??

While we're on the topic of myths and misconceptions, however, allow me to relay to you a conversation Radek (R) had with an Arabic Christian anti-Semitic cab driver (ACASCD). Due to the large crucifix hanging in his taxi, Radek asked him if he is a Christian. This started the conversation.

ACASCD: *"Jews have black hearts!"*

R: *"You know, my wife is Jewish, and she doesn't have a black heart, and I know many other Jews that also don't happen to have black hearts."*

ACASCD: *"But the Jews killed Jesus."*

R: *"No, you killed him, I killed him, Jesus willingly laid down his life for all of our sins."*

> **"Therefore My Father loves Me, because I lay down My life that I may take it again. No one takes it from Me, but I lay it down of Myself."** (John 10:17, 18)

Jesus prophesied that He would be handed over to the Gentiles who would crucify Him.

> **"For He will be delivered to the Gentiles and will be mocked and insulted and spit upon. They will scourge Him and kill Him."**
> (Luke 18:32, 33)

It was the Jews and Gentiles together who were responsible for Jesus' death, which gave us a place in a covenant of salvation with God. (Acts 4:27, Eph. 2:11-13)

R: *"Anyways, as a Christian, you should have the attitude that was in Ruth towards the people of Israel."*
ACASCD: *"Who is Ruth?"*
R: *"Didn't you read the book of Ruth in the Old Testament?"*
ACASCD: *"I only read the NEW Testament!!"*
R: *"Then you don't know the foundation of your faith."*

Bedtime and Bullets

While reading bedtime stories to Shmuel, I thought I distinctly heard the rapid, continuous sound of machine gun fire, followed by several loud blasts. I tried to ignore them, rationalize them away as something else. Surely no one is actually shooting outside our bedroom window! Shmuel is so used to these sounds that he barely notices anymore, except for a casual comment, *"Hmm, I wonder if that's firecrackers or shooting, Mom?"* Sure enough, the next day reported machine gun firing and rocket blasts heard all over Jerusalem at 8:00 P.M. Somehow, it just doesn't seem real. Maybe having grown up on too much T.V. makes the violence seem like a make-believe scene, rather than real people getting shot with real bullets.

What A Mess!

Shalom from Jerusalem - and what a mess this city is! Due to the general strike, piles of messy, stinking garbage is accumulating on the sidewalks and alleyways of Jerusalem. Shvitah (strike) was one of the first new Hebrew words we learned. Today, as Liat and I went for a walk, we noticed several of the green plastic bins had been torched, (probably by vandals) their gooey, melted and charred plastic adding to the general ugliness of the street. Does this symbolically portray the spiritual condition of this city and the nation of Israel at this time? Is the Holy Spirit giving the people of Israel a graphic word picture?

We know that this nation is defiled and living in deep darkness, but we also know that in the midst of the darkness, a light has dawned.

> **"Arise, shine (kumi, ori) For your light has come! And the glory of the Lord is risen upon you. For behold, the darkness shall cover the earth, and deep darkness the people, but the Lord will arise over you and His glory will be seen upon you."** (Is. 60:1, 2)

> **"The people who walked in darkness have seen a great light, those who dwelt in the land of the shadow of death; Upon them a light has shined."** (Isa. 9:2)

Glimpses of Jerusalem

You have most likely heard of the continued violence in Jerusalem and around Israel. A police vehicle could never negotiate its way through the narrow, cobblestone streets and alleyways of the Old City, therefore many police ride horseback, khaki helmets strapped to the flanks of their horses. As I walked to school to pick up Shmuel, I noticed a simple, plastic drinking bottle sitting on a post on the sidewalk. Normally, this would not be a cause for concern, but living in a city besieged by terrorists, one must be ever on the alert. I wondered if I should bring this to someone's attention, but someone else beat me to it. She noticed the bottle as well, and immediately notified the military standing at their post nearby who came to check it out. At bus stops, every bag and suitcase must be accounted for. If a bag is found that no one can claim, the entire depot must be cleared of people while the bomb squad comes to check out the 'suspicious object'. You get used to people always asking you if this or that bag belongs to you. At the entrance to every mall and public place is a guard who searches through your handbags for anything suspicious. Buses that must travel through the territories are equipped with steel grating over their windshields and double paned glass all around to guard against snipers and rocks. This is so different than what we are used to, where the question of whether or not a bomb might go off in your vicinity is not something that ordinarily enters our nice Canadian minds.

Israeli Transportation Trivia

- Cars don't automatically stop for pedestrians on Israeli streets. You better be quick!
- Buses don't give transfers. New bus, new ticket.
- If the taxi doesn't turn on his meter (called a moneh) at the beginning of the trip, you don't have to pay him. Most prefer to 'make a deal'.
- An inch is considered ample clearance by most Israeli drivers.
- If the lane you want doesn't exist, Israeli driving customs indicate you just create your own

- Directional signs are few and far between. Come with the homing instincts of a pigeon or resign yourself to becoming lost - often.
- Those with weak stomachs or a tendency to motion sickness may want to bring a discreet 'bag' while riding Israeli buses on the winding, bumpy roadways.
- Sidewalks are legitimate (apparently) parking places for cars in Israeli cities
- Car alarms going off loudly usually mean nothing
- Israelis use their car horn like their voices – loud and often!

Enjoy travelling this beautiful land, upon which the Lord cares for continually.

Struggling with Everyday Living – Gas!

All of us, at times, struggle for the blessing. We are coming to know and finally accept, however, that almost all things here in Israel are a struggle - it is the very nature of the nation and the meaning of its name. Even the simplest things require great perseverance. Take for example the gas. Last week they cut off our gas. Not that we hadn't paid our bill, but they wanted to fix something or other and therefore cut off the gas to get our attention on this matter. Since the stoves are gas, this means no cooking until it is re-connected. With a baby and little boy in the house, this was terribly inconvenient, to say the least. And so, the struggle began in earnest.

Day one: All the first day was spent just trying to get through on the phone number written on the notice. Finally, in the evening, someone answered, giving me a different number to call in the morning.

Day two: - Wasted the morning trying to get through on this second line and my persistence was finally rewarded with a human voice. But only for a few seconds - my call was transferred and the connection promptly cut off! This occurred several times. Once, a man answered who actually asked for a few details. I thought, aha, now we're getting somewhere. I had new hope -- until I heard those dreaded words: *"I'm going to transfer you."*

"NOOOOOOOOO!" I screamed into the phone, *"DON'T CUT ME OFF AGAIN!!!!!!!!!!"* But my pleading fell upon deaf ears - too late 'click'.

In tears of anger and frustration, I told Radek that we were just going to have to learn to live on cold cornflakes and milk. Two heads are sometimes better than one, and so together we came up with the idea to call our landlady. Being the kind woman that she is, she took it upon herself to get through to the gas people. Also unable to get through on the line, she went down in person. We received a call that someone would come that day to re-connect our gas, but no one came.

Day three: Still no one came. Our landlady called to check and said that she would go down there again if our gas was not connected that day. By evening, we had given up on hot food, but lo and behold, at 9:30 P.M., we answered the buzzer to the apartment and hear a voice say,

   "Gas man here".

   Only in Israel....

How Much Money Do You Really Have??

<u>Toy Store:</u> One day, Courtney went looking for a small toy to bring home as a gift for her little brother, Timothy. She browsed outside the store where several small toys were displayed.

Store clerk: *"Can I help you?"*
Courtney: *"No, thank you, I'm just looking."*
Clerk: *"Well, what are you looking for?"*
Courtney: *"Just a little toy for my brother."*
Clerk: *"How much money do you have?"*
Courtney: (feeling pressured now) *"Ahh, well, I have about ten sheckels to spend."*
Clerk: *"O.K. all the 10 sheckel toys are out here."*
Courtney goes to look inside the store. The clerk runs after her, shouting, *"Don't go in there! There's nothing in there you want!"*
Courtney: *"Well, I would just like to look around in here if you don't mind."*
Clerk: *"No, no, there's nothing here under ten sheckels."*
Courtney: (indignant) *"Maybe I want to spend more than ten sheckels!"*
Clerk: (looking down at her and speaking as a mother to a naughty child) *"Oh, ...so you DO have more than ten sheckels!"* ☺

Let Me See in Your Wallet

Radek and I stood at the grocery cashier clerk's station with a whole line up of people behind us. When the cashier finished ringing up the groceries, Radek gave her a large bill. The cashier said, *"Do you have anything smaller?"* Radek, without checking and not wanting the hassle, just said no. The woman next to us in line actually reached over, poked her finger in Radek's wallet and pointed to his cash.

"Oh, there's a smaller bill", she said – to our amazement and chagrin.

Another Toy Story

We went looking for a cheap pair of kids sunglasses for Timothy for the summer. Did I say cheap? In Israel? We went into a toy store and asked if he had any children's sunglasses. No, he said, you should go to the optometrist. We explained that we were only looking for toy sunglasses, not real ones from the optometrist. Toys? the clerk asks, raising his eyebrows. Toys? We don't sell toys here. Go figure...

Chocolate Covered Raisins – Israeli Retailing

While pregnant, I often experienced cravings, which my family tried their best to satisfy. One of the things that I loved when pregnant was chocolate covered orange peels and raisins. Courtney passed a stand of chocolates and nuts on her way home one day and decided to bring me home a little surprise. She asked the clerk, *"Sir, do you have any chocolate covered raisins?"*

"No," he replied. Courtney looked over at the shelves and spied what she thought looked like chocolate covered raisins.

"Are you sure you don't have chocolate covered raisins?", Courtney asked.

"No," he answered again most definitely.

"Ah...do you mind if I just sample one of these little chocolates over here, sir?" Courtney asked hesitantly.

"Sure, go ahead." the clerk replied. Yes, indeed, these were definitely chocolate covered raisins, Courtney confirmed as she bit into one. *"Humph...."* was the retailer's only response.

More Retail Israeli style

Radek went to buy a package of two AA batteries. The clerk gave him a four pack and said that will be twenty four sheckels. Radek said: *"No, I just want a two pack."*
"O.K., no problem (ain ba'aya)", says the clerk. He promptly pulls out a pair of scissors, snips the package in half and says,
"That will be twelve sheckels."

Your Kids are our Kids

When I had a baby in Israel, I found out that my child no longer belongs to me but to the whole Israeli Jewish community, which they seem quick to point out. Everyone has child care advice (unsolicited of course). The first time we took the baby out to the grocery store she was one month old. What we didn't know is that Israelis are not in the custom of taking their babies to the grocery stores at that age.
"How old is the baby?" The butcher at the meat counter asked.
"One month." We replied.
"Tsk, tsk,", he vocalized as he shook his head in bewilderment, saying, *"Loh normally! (not normal),"*
When we took the baby out for a stroll in a huge pram that we bought second hand, we found that by three or four months old, she no longer liked to lie down for her walks but preferred to sit up so she could see around her. (She's a very inquisitive child). So we started taking her out in a stroller which we would put blankets in and around her to hold her little body snugly. Invariably, someone would stop us and say,
"What are you doing?! That is terrible for the baby's back! You have to put her in a pram so she can lie down." No amount of assurance that I had raised three other children in such a fashion would calm them and so we learned to

always agree with them and then go about our merry way.

People often told me I had the baby overdressed or underdressed, that her fingernails were too long, that I shouldn't let the baby play with this or that, or that I should be careful that she doesn't bump her head...Finally, instead of resenting their interference, I came to understand and love the fact that people here care so much about their children, as precocious as so many of them are. They are indulged when young, since most will have to enter the army when they are grown. Israeli children are very precious to the community, because of the precariousness of life here and so we share one another's responsibility in raising and watching over these little ones.

Kotel Etiquette

When visiting the Western (Wailing) Wall, called the Kotel, there are a few things to keep in mind. First of all, men and women are segregated – so please head to the right section. Secondly, women should be modestly dressed in respect for the holiness of the site. Modest to us is not necessarily modest to them. It means a dress or skirt and blouse with legs, chest, arms, and head covered. Once, I wore a long dress with sleeves and covered my hair. A woman came up and rebuked me for my immodesty.

"*What is not covered?*" I asked in amazement.

"*Your chest.*" she replied with a look like, 'as if you didn't know'. Not that my dress was low cut, but yes, I have to admit, an extension of my neck was exposed. Oye!

It's not always that bad.

Begging in Israel

Many beggars line the gates, streets and stairways of the Old City, included the path to the Wall. It's between you and the Holy Spirit who you give to and how much, but keep in mind, if you give it all away to the ones on the stairs, you are going to have nothing left for all the pathetic old widows at the Wall itself who ask for tzedkah (charity) for this or that organization or home for the poor, blind, homeless or other such misfortune. Autistic children seems to be a favorite for home collections. I don't mean to sound disrespectful, but it seems like all those who come to my door collecting for charity ask for it for autistic children. How many autistic children can there be in Israel? Begging is almost a respected profession in Israel. Charity boxes are found even attached to bus stops where you can deposit your offering for the poor and hungry. Giving to the poor is a well-respected principle in Israel and so the beggars can be quite bold. Sometimes they come with a specific need to your home, especially before shabbat when it is a mitzvah (good deed) to give before the sabbath. One man came with a story that he needed money for medical bills. He had with him a photocopy of his bills in a neat plastic covering as he went door to door. O.K., I thought, I'll give him the benefit of the doubt and I handed him an offering. He looked at it and said, *"You could write me a cheque"*. Seriously! Even when I told him I would rather give him the sheckels, he still tried to convince me to write out a cheque for the full amount that he assured me he would pay back. Right...

One old woman on the stairway to the Kotel was downright brazen. She begged for some charity, so I gave her a ten sheckel coin, knowing I would give more at the Wall itself. The old, toothless beggar woman protested,

"No, No, give me bills!"

I said no thank you and walked on. She screamed out after me, *"Loh yaffe, g'veret! Loh yaffe!"* which roughly translated means, *"Not nice, lady, not nice!"*

I heard her voice shrieking after me for a long, long ways. Since she is a regular, at that spot, I usually try to find an alternate route to the Wall now.

Once you arrive at the Wall, the main event is to actually touch the ancient stones or to kiss them even and to put your prayer request on a little folded piece of paper in the cracks of the wall. Legend has it that it is the poor of Jerusalem that built this section of the Wall and that is why God didn't have the heart to destroy it. King Solomon prayed that if anyone, even a foreigner would come and pray at this place that God would hear their prayers and forgive them and give them victory in the battle. We've seen people come from all around the world, just to bring their prayer request to stuff in a crack. You may have to push a bit to actually get to the Wall, depending on how crowded it is. The women can watch the men's section from a dividing wall behind it. Bar Mitzvahs and weddings often take place at the Kotel which are a joy to behold.

The men chant, pray, dance, and blow the shofar. Often the festivals are celebrated here. Calls for corporate prayer sometimes go out to the Jewish community of Jerusalem and Israel to come to the Wall to pray in times of crisis or emergency. Tens of thousands sometimes come. On a regular day, it is usually easy to get to the Wall itself and be prepared, it is usually a highly charged emotional and spiritual experience, as the presence of God actually hovers there.

Timothy blowing the shofar.

Have your dollars ready for the old Babas with their hands out, but they may sometimes in their eagerness come at you all at once. Usually they are quite polite and appreciative and speak a blessing over you.

Caution: The Red Cord

Beggars or charity collectors at the Wall and other places sometimes try to place a red cord on your wrist and recite a blessing after you have given to them. DON'T ACCEPT IT! Although you may think this is neat and spiritual, the red cord actually has its roots in Jewish mysticism and paganism.

A rabbi trying to give us the red cord.

Backing out

When you have finished praying (and weeping), don't turn your back and walk away. Just as lawyers do not turn their backs on a judge in a courtroom when they leave, but rather back out, facing him or her, the custom is to do the same at the Wall. Face the wall, backing up (with quick checks behind you so that you don't run some poor baba over) until you reach the end of the courtyard, at which time you can turn around and be on your way, basking in the glow of this Holy Place, the Kotel.

The Kotel (Western Wall)

From the Holy to the Profane: Israeli Toilet Culture

Israeli toilet culture is quite a change from what we are accustomed to in Canada. Radek and I have decided upon a rating system for public toilets in Israel from 1-10, with points given for cleanliness and for each 'luxury item' supplied (toilet paper, toilet seat, lock on door, door, etc).

Toilet facilities range all the way from those with no toilet seat, no lock on the door, and no paper, with mud and gunk all over the floor such as at the circus, to clean, posh facilities in the five star hotels with everything supplied. (Which is why we love visiting hotels!)

Because paper products such as kleenex are so expensive in Israel, toilet paper is used instead. The first time I saw a woman haul a whole roll of toilet paper out of her purse, I considered this bizarre. But now I find myself sticking my own roll in my purse when I go out.

Toilet culture is a bit of a shock for us Canadians, especially with regards to the children. Children are allowed to 'pee' practically anywhere at any time, even in public places. This is of necessity, since toilet facilities are often few and far between. But the first time I saw a parent pull down their child's pants for him to pee on a tree in the middle of the shook *(marketplace), I did a double take, I must admit. Just yesterday, three little boys pulled down their pants in the middle of the playground and peed on the same tree simultaneously. Where's a camera when you need one? In one of the most amusing 'toilet incidents', a father had one of his children pee off the ping pong table he was standing on, while the other child stood, peeing on the ground below. Of course the unfortunate child below got 'sprayed' which led to a terrible row (with their pants down). The word 'pee', by the way, is used in 'adult talk' in Hebrew. Really! I went for an ultrasound, and the nurse came out and asked me in Hebrew if I would go and 'pee pee'. I looked at her – but she was completely serious. I later came to understand that this is just part of Israeli 'toilet culture'.

Conclusion

Here we are, it seems, at the conclusion of a book about the 'Holy Land' - talking toilets! It seems quite irreverent to end a book on Israel on such an 'earthy' note, but then perhaps it is strangely appropriate. For this is a land where we come with hopes and dreams and romanticized notions of 'living in God's special land'. We come with scriptures and ideals, and end up rating the toilets. When we discovered that not everything is 'kosher' in our Jewish homeland, we began to wonder at times, what we are doing here and if we had 'missed God' and made a terrible mistake. Some people never get past this stage, and live here in a state of depression, or become critical of the Land, spreading 'evil reports' and causing others to also lose heart. As is evident from this book, this is a place that challenges our petty, egocentric, selfish demands that 'everything go our way' - because everything usually does NOT go our way at all. For 'control freaks', those who need to be in control of people and situations to feel secure, the pain of crucifying this fleshly habit can be excruciating. This land tests our hearts and our characters. It stretches us beyond the point that we thought we could bear. We are commanded to love our God with all of our hearts and souls; but there is only one thing in the entire Bible that God says He will do with all of His heart and soul – and that one thing is this:

> **"Yes, I will rejoice over them to do them good, and I will assuredly plant them in this land, with all My heart and with all My soul."** (Jer. 32:41)

I welcome you also to visit, to taste and see that the Lord is good, and even for those who are able, to 'come home'. For those who cannot now come, please stand with us and with all of Israel to see God's great purposes come to pass in this special Land.

Shalom
With love in Yeshua,

Hannah

Postscript (March 24th, 2008)

YOU SHALL KNOW THE TRUTH AND THE TRUTH SHALL MAKE YOU FREE!

Since I began to write this book, several years have passed; almost a decade in fact. So much has taken place – enough to write another book. Perhaps one day I will. But for now I will try to be brief, just updating you with the highlights. I would love to leave you with this funny, cheerful, lighthearted view of Israel, and with a perception of us as courageous pioneers of faith like Joshua and Caleb who sacrifice everything to take our place in the Promised Land, who face all the giants like the mighty David and who stick it out through thick and thin like Job saying, "Though you slay me, yet will I trust You". I wish I could leave you thinking of us like that. Except for this one thing – integrity. Maybe it's this troublesome prayer that I prayed long ago, "Lord, keep lies and falsehood far from me." It doesn't allow me to pretend. We have had to…I should say, *I* have had to face some hard and painful truths about myself, about Israel, and about journeying with God. It is this conclusion to our journey that I would now like to share with you. Because I believe that when we take off our masks and get real, then other people are also free to remove their masks. When we share, not only our victories and mountain top experiences, but also our disappointments and our failures, then others may be set free to tell the truth as well. Yeshua said that we shall know the truth and the truth shall set us free. (John 8:32) Here's to truth and freedom! Hallelulyah!

Cracks in the Foundation

In the summer of 2001, we left Jerusalem for a whirlwind tour of speaking in various places in the United States and Canada. We flew with our son, Timothy, age 8, and daughter, Liat, age 2, in over 23 flights and many hours of driving. And I was sick as a dog. Just before leaving Israel, I contracted a serious virus that infected my mouth. It was full of painful sores so severe that I could barely drink water. And in all of this, I was preaching and speaking nearly every day. Instead of taking time for our family to enjoy some of the sights and attractions, we were driven hard from one place to another. What drove us so relentlessly? Surely not the Holy Spirit, who cautions to be gentle when travelling with little ones, not to overdrive the herd. I'll never forget driving through Orlando, Florida. Most families would enjoy the opportunity to take their children to Disneyworld, SeaWorld, Nassau Space Centre and all these cool places for kids. But instead, we raced through to the next destination. I was so sick that I had to cancel a meeting I had scheduled about publishing my books and Liat threw up all over me. Of course I had no change of clothes so had to travel, in pain and covered with baby vomit for the whole trip. Cracks in the foundation of our marriage and ministry were beginning to show. When we got back to Jerusalem, things did not improve. Radek used 'avoidance' as a defense strategy, which caused me to feel unloved, which caused my emotions to escalate, which only served to cause further withdrawal and shutdown on Radek's part. We became more and more alienated from one another. I suffered another two miscarriages and hemorrhaged, having to be hospitalized on Liat's one year birthday. A year before to the day, the Lord had given me a beautiful baby girl; and that day, he had taken one away. I came to a place of saying, *"He gives and takes away; blessed be the name of the Lord."* I felt disappointed and not cherished as a woman. I was started to feel like a fading flower, wilting for lack of water, sunlight and the nourishment I needed which was love, affirmation, attention and acceptance. I had not yet learned to lean on the Lord totally and trust Him alone to meet all of my needs in complete dependence.

Although hurting emotionally and spiritually inside, I felt that I could not slow down and process what was happening in my soul, in my marriage and in my relationship with God. 'Ministry' became the driving force of our lives, not the Holy Spirit. We depended on our supporters financially, since my husband could not work without a visa, and so it began to come down to the money. The newsletters had to be sent out each month because we needed the support coming in. I began to feel convicted that I was no longer walking in my integrity; that I was becoming a hypocrite – presenting myself as one thing but behind closed doors, it was another thing entirely. We began to see 'Israel' as the focus and not the Lord. We became more and more 'religious' and legalistic, even believing the viewpoint that I did not have the right to decide my own fertility but had to leave that in God's hands too. I did not stop to consider that God's word also speaks against divorce and re-marriage as well; so we stopped using any kind of birth control and adopted a fatalistic attitude that 'If God wants me to get pregnant I will and if He doesn't I won't. We just went ahead in blind faith, ignoring the high risks of childbirth at my age. I began to feel more and more that my life was out of control; that I had no choices over my life. I felt that I 'had to' perform, 'had to' speak, 'had to' write, 'had to' be a good wife and mother and 'had to' allow myself to become pregnant again. Most of all, I felt that I 'had to' keep up the façade of a super spiritual family serving the Lord in the esteemed Land of Israel. Privately, I kept thinking that if people really knew us, they would never support us.

Two things happened to move us out of Jerusalem, and ultimately out of the Land. The first factor was that I got pregnant again (no surprise) and we knew I would not for very much longer be able to walk up the four flights of stairs carrying a baby, a stroller and bags of groceries. We looked for another apartment, but were tired of being squished into cramped quarters apartment and did not look forward to squeezing in another child. Larger living quarters were of course more expensive and we did not have the faith to believe that we could afford the higher rent. This was probably a lie, but I think we were also looking for an excuse to get out of Jerusalem. We were tired of living in the city and longed to find God in a simpler, quieter, more peaceful place in nature. My husband was especially stressed in Jerusalem – the noise, the traffic, the crowded conditions – all seemed to push him to the brink. I felt that I couldn't live with his reactivity any longer, so we looked around and decided that it was to the wide open spaces of the Negev (desert) that we would move. Here we could rent a whole house with land and a horse in the back for less than what we paid for our apartment in Jerusalem. I had my reservations: what about the children's education? How would they cope in a public Israeli school again? How could we leave the Messianic school? What about fellowship? How would we leave the congregation? But all this didn't seem to matter; when my husband set his mind on something, no amount of nagging or arguing could change it. We were both operating more and more in the natural realm of the flesh rather than listening to the Holy Spirit. Ignoring my lack of peace, and wanting to be a good, submissive wife, I agreed to move – with one stipulation – air conditioning.

So we moved to the Negev, into the middle of the Israeli desert, to a lovely large five bedroom home - in July, the hottest month of the year, with temperatures soaring way above 40 degrees - and me six months pregnant – and no air conditioning. Oops. My husband forgot this little detail when choosing a home. And in Israel, it's not like you can just walk into any old store and pick up an air conditioning unit for a cheap price. It was a big deal. Radek chose this moment to take a stand – at my expense – to say that he would not buy an air conditioning unit until the Israeli government agreed to

Postscript

give him a work visa. He didn't want to spend the money if we would not be staying. I had never experienced that kind of heat in my life! Nor the flies! I thought I was going to die of suffocation. All I could do was sit in front of a fan that our landlords mercifully lent us. I could not move. As soon as I moved away from the fan, I began to sweat profusely and could not breathe. I begged, I pleaded, I nagged, I screamed, I wept; I did everything I knew to do (and yes, I prayed), but my husband would not budge his position.

I will never forget the moment I decided that I had to move or die. Surrounded by boxes and unable to unpack my new home, I knew that I at least needed to find the toilet paper.

Our home in the Negev.

So I ran to the bathroom, filled up the sink with cold water, dunked my head in it and then went searching for the box that contained toilet paper. I would run back after a few seconds and dunk again. This went on and on, until I fell to the floor, weeping, face drenched with tears, sweat, snot, and who knows what else, crying out to God to save me! Feeling that my only hope would be to get to water, and knowing that there was a pool on a nearby moshav (village), I marched into the room where my husband was sleeping and demanded the keys to the van. Friends of ours had donated to us a nine-seater van! The fact that I did not have an Israeli driver's license made no matter to me now. It was do or die! When Radek saw the look on my face, he knew better than to argue. "Get your bathing suits, kids" I hollered. "We're going swimming!" "But Mom", they cried, "You don't know how to drive." When they saw that same look on my face, they just grabbed their suits and towels and jumped into the van, eyes bugged out and scared. Narrowly missing the rubber plant and cactus, I zoomed down the desert's back roads until I reached the pool. Halleuyah! Relief! We drove every day to that pool as my body got more and more pregnant – it was how we survived.

The pool in the Negev.

Friends of ours phoned from Canada and when they found out what was going on, said that he should know he is endangering not only my life but the life of our unborn child. Although he eventually relented and bought an air conditioning unit, bitter seeds of resentment and even hatred were taking root in my heart. Although the clerk who sold us an air conditioner assured us on the life of his firstborn son that we would have that unit installed the very next day, it took a whole week before the installers actually made it out to our house. First they were scared to come (we lived only a couple of kilometers from Gaza and Egypt); then it was some kind of Jewish holiday and they claimed to be religious. Who knows?! This is Israel! God was really working on my flesh in the Negev, that's all I can say.

One act of God's mercy and grace was evident in the faithfulness of our friends, Colin and Rosie, from Jerusalem. They travelled every other weekend with their children to stay with us, to fellowship and worship with us and to pray with and for us. Colin prayer walked the moshav until the wee hours of the morning, braving dog attacks, terrorist attacks and who know what else, in order to see God's purposes unfold for us and for the people of this area. We were shocked to find the Negev a place of serpents and scorpions in more than one sense of the word. We went to a children's gathering that was supposed to be a show about animals. Instead, they played heavy rock music and the entertainer walked scorpions across his face and draped serpents around the children's neck. Oye! We met many precious people in the Negev and God did give us many opportunities to share the gospel message – even with the IDF. One day, some Israeli soldiers came, asking Radek if he would make a movie about the underground tunnels for the IDF. They had heard of his excellent skills as a video editor and he was thrilled to help them. We ordered pizza and they stayed up all night working on this project. In the morning, we found them all sacked out, sound asleep, all over the floor. Radek, as usual, never lost an opportunity to share the gospel with anyone and these young soldiers were keenly interested to hear about the Messiah. Radek carried an incredible anointing as an evangelist – absolutely no fear of man. He would witness to anyone – from the most religious 'black hat'[53] in Jerusalem to the most wicked secular sinner.

---

53 Black hat is a term used to refer to the Orthodox religious Jews who wear black hats and black suits.

He would also pick up hitchhikers in our nine-seater van where we kept Messianic material and Bibles in Hebrew to give out to them. I am quite sure that the enemy of our souls did not like what we were doing in this region of the country. And so he declared war. I will never forget the day I received notice. I woke up one morning and walked out the front door where we kept a large barrel to catch the rain water. Inside the rain barrel was a huge, ugly, dead lizard; in my spirit I knew we needed to prepare for a huge battle. I didn't know then that it would be a battle for my life and the life of my unborn child.

As we approached the time of delivery (which we had planned with a midwife for a home birth), I received a call from my older sister in Canada. She is an Orthodox Jewess and certainly does not agree with my beliefs, but has always been supportive of me as a loving and gentle sister. "Are you in okay?" my sister asked. "Are you in labor?" "Yes"... and "No" I answered. She explained that she had such a strong sense that she needed to call me at that exact moment. I assured her that everything was fine and we chatted for a few minutes before I hung up. I stood up to hang up the phone and felt a rush of warm liquid run down my legs. "Oh, my water broke!", I thought. Better call the midwife. "Liat!", I called, "Tell Daddy that Mommy's water broke." Excited, but not really understanding what I meant, she ran to relay the message. It was then that I looked down and saw that the liquid was bright red. And it wasn't just trickling; it was like a gushing river. My first thought was, "Funny, I don't remember it being red when my water broke before..." So I called my midwife and when I casually mentioned this, she spoke with a tone of strident urgency in her voice, "Call an ambulance – now!" By the time the ambulance attendants arrived, I had lay semi-conscious and naked, in a pool of my own blood in the shower. Their faces went white as they hustled me into the ambulance on a stretcher and connected me to oxygen. I thought of only two things: "Don't let Liat see them take me away" and 'I never said goodbye." I could hear them radio ahead for an ICU ambulance to be dispatched to meet us on the highway. We were at least an hour from the nearest hospital and I knew they thought they would lose me and the baby. But as mysteriously as the bleeding started, it also stopped in the ambulance. Even my mid-wife, who is an agnostic Jew, said she had to admit it was a miracle from God.

Something had gone wrong in the pregnancy and the tests showed my organs beginning to lose strength; the doctors wanted to perform an emergency caesarian. I was absolutely opposed! This was Ms. Natural Childbirth here. I had no idea that I had so much pride invested in my ability to bear children without medical intervention. With my prior medical experience, I avoided doctors like the plague! And now here I was at their mercy it seemed. They agreed to give me that one night to decide. All night I prayed, and prayed and prayed....I begged God to intervene and do another miracle. But in the morning, my medical signs were even worse and they said there was no choice but to perform the caesarian. I turned my face to the wall and wept long and hard. To say that I was terrified would be an understatement; they had to perform the surgery under a general anesthetic because I couldn't stop shaking enough for the epidural to be administered. I'm not sure exactly what happened during that surgery in that Israeli desert hospital, but my body, soul, and spirit has never been the same since. I thank God for my beautiful baby boy we named Avi-ad, from Isaiah 9:6, one of the names of the Messiah meaning 'my everlasting Father'. He was born November 6th, 2002. Today, Avi-ad is five years old and is a healthy, happy, spunky, funny little guy. He also has one of the most caring, most compassionate hearts that I have ever experienced in any child or adult. What a special gift he is to me in the 'late afternoon' of my life.

Avi-ad

But we got off to a rocky start, that's for sure. I lost so much blood that I became anemic. I was probably in no way, shape or form, ready to go home when they released me, but this hospital was so overcrowded because of the Bedouin's high fertility rate, that they needed the bed. They wheeled me out on a rickety, one-legged wheelchair and the whole ride home was absolute agony.

But God sent me two saving graces in the form of two women who saved my life. One was Jennifer, a young woman from Texas, whose family we met and visited while on tour in 2001. Jennifer had called me one day out of the blue during my pregnancy and said she had a dream. In her dream, she saw me sitting atop a pile of sand dunes, weeping, and she heard a voice say, "Go to Hannah. She will have need of you." So, at the risk of sounding crazy (we barely knew each other), she asked if I wanted her to come and stay with me. As usual, with a 'the more the merrier' kind of lighthearted attitude, I agreed, not knowing that her presence with me at Avi-ad's birth probably made all the difference between life and death. Jennifer stayed with me 24/7 while

I lay on that hospital bed, caring for me and the baby. She brought me food (okay, okay, so she mixed up the dairy and the meat trays, destroying the whole kosher system of the hospital kitchen ☺); she brought the baby to me to nurse and helped wipe and clean and dress him. In this hospital, there were no baby wipes. When Jennifer asked what to wipe his dirty bottom with, the nurses said to use his soiled pajamas. Oye. We had to search hard just for a pillow and bring our own painkillers! In all of this, the best thing that Jennifer did was to keep me laughing. She had this great sense of humor and even though my stitches hurt, I couldn't help but laugh at her jokes and stories. She refused to leave me and Avi, and when the hospital wouldn't give her a mat or cot, she just lay on the bare floor to sleep beside my bed.

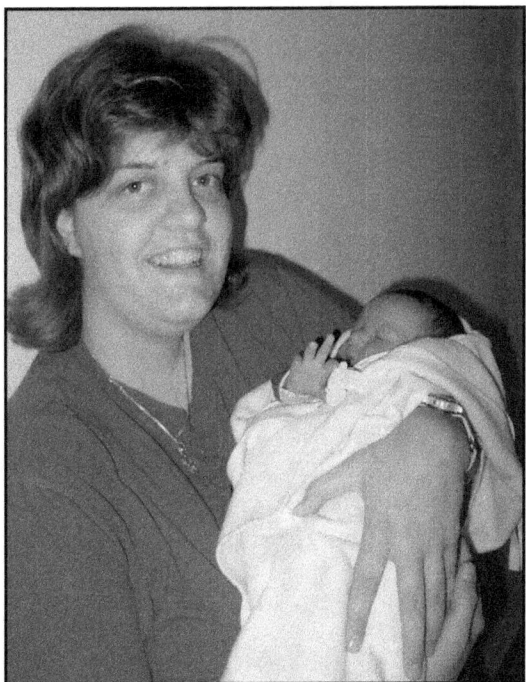

Jennifer holding Avi.

God sent another woman into my household and she remains forever in my heart. Her name is Assiah, and she was a new immigrant from Khazhakstan, living in the Negev of Israel. She came to cook and keep the house until I could get back up on my feet. We didn't know it would take so long. But Assiah kept us all alive and fed. The fact that she could not speak much English or Hebrew and I could not speak much Russian didn't seem to matter. We grew to love one another. Later, when I ran out of money to pay her, she refused to quit and kept caring for me for free. Israelis had called her a 'Dirty Russian', knocked over her sewing machines that she used to try and make a living, had slapped her and cut off her water supply when she couldn't pay the bill. But my Assiah was a saint; she also was a Christian and we would pray together. One day, I lay there thinking of how much I would love someone to come and massage my feet as they were so swollen. Within a couple of minutes, Assiah was in the room, kneeling by my bed, massaging my feet. How I loved her – and still do – I just can't find her anymore. She moved away to Eilat last I heard and I haven't been able to locate her again.

Assiah

Postscript

This crisis did not end, however, once home from the hospital. Although on heavy doses of painkillers, the pain did not lessen. In fact, it seemed to be getting worse. Also, I was developing a fever and discharge; feeling weaker and weaker by the day. We met my midwife at the hospital and the doctor examined me to find that I had a uterine infection and severe anemia. It was a long road to recovery, one that I am still on today, the recovery of one's health and strength. But what was most wounded was my faith and my confidence – in myself, in my husband's love for me and at times, in God Himself. Why was He allowing this to happen in my life?

Our situation went from bad to worse when Radek went to check on his visa status at the Ministry of the Interior's branch office in Be'er Sheva. They gave him fourteen days to leave the country. All of us walked around in shock – not believing that we could be evicted from our own land. Aviad was only a few months old and on top of it all, Jennifer contracted a serious virus which entered her blood and she almost died. Yes, the enemy had declared war; and it seemed that he was winning the battle by defeating the saints. We did not have the strength or the financial resources anymore to enter into a legal battle with the government of Israel. We got rid of everything – a five bedroom house full of furniture – all our belongings and possessions. We gave most of it to the poor Thai workers that lived in little shacks in the village and worked in the hot greenhouses. Our landlords tried to talk my husband into storing the best of the furniture in case we changed our mind and came back – but we thought we would never be back.

As my Mom used to say, "People plan and God laughs."

Back to Exile

Not knowing where else to go, still sick and weak from such a traumatic childbirth, we returned in May of 2003 to my home town in Canada – like dogs with our tails between our legs. We had been soundly whipped, defeated. Never mind that our pastor prayed over us and said, "You have not failed". We felt like utter losers. I fell into a deep depression. Radek responded in his typical 'avoid and don't deal with it' manner and went back to work driving a taxi so that he would be gone 24/7. I bore the burden alone, without his partnership or support. Even though my family was happy to see me and have me back, I felt totally and utterly lost, alone and abandoned. I was, at times, so physically weak that I could not walk up the stairs of the dumpy townhouse we rented but actually had to crawl. In my weakened emotional and physical condition, I could not cope on my own with the demands of a newborn baby and an active, emotionally demanding two year old as well as pre-adolescent. I would sometimes lock myself in the bathroom and just scream in utter rage, frustration, and pain. I was afraid of what I might do to myself or to the children. I would often come down in the middle of the night (Radek worked all night), prostrate myself face down on the floor and weep until I had no strength left to weep, crying out to God. But all I heard in return was a deafening silence. I had no one I could talk to and process my feelings of loss and grief. When I mentioned that we had returned from Israel, people in the Church looked at me like I had just said I returned from the moon. No one seemed to have a clue what this meant in my life. I struggled with bitterness and unforgiveness; I felt like I had let everyone down who had supported us in the ministry and cared about us so much when Avi-ad was born. So many precious people prayed and sent gifts for the babies. They had so much more grace for me than what I had for myself. We tried to put the past behind us and move on; make the best of things.

Radek took training and tried several new vocations: real estate, life insurance, even truck driving, but nothing seemed to work out. I started teaching some Hebrew classes. We even changed our names so that we would all have the same last name. Since my maiden name means eagle, we chose the Hebrew word for eagle which is Nesher. We claimed the scripture that as we would wait upon the Lord, hoping in His mercy, He would cause us to rise up again, out of the ashes of our circumstances, as an eagle to soar high above the winds. Radek also chose a Canadian name, David, desiring to be a man after God's own heart and to leave his Polish roots and dysfunctional past behind. If only it could be done so easily by changing our name, our job, or any other external circumstance. But the real change needed was inside – a new heart and a right spirit within us.

Besides our serious marital difficulties, we also struggled financially. I was not well enough to work and wanted to stay home with my babies and Radek could not support the family even though he worked long hours on a taxi drivers salary. Creditors were calling and bills mounting. I heard Radek (now David) begin to talk about how we made a mistake in leaving Israel so easily without at least a fight. He watched one of my videos again about Ruth, who refused to leave Naomi, a prophetic message to the Church about standing with Israel.[54] He said the Holy Spirit spoke to him through this message that we were wrong to leave Israel and even if they asked us to leave we should have said like Ruth, "Do not ask me to leave you....". We were afraid that, like Naomi, we would lose everything because of leaving the Land. No one could seem to understand how we felt about this. When David asked if I would be willing to go back to Israel, I said, "No Way!!!" And I added that there's no way we could go back anyways because we have no money

---

54 See Ruth a Righteous Gentile, DVD on our website:

to do so. So he issued me a challenge: "If God somehow, supernaturally, miraculously, provided for tickets for all five of us to return to the Land, then would you consider it?" I laughed (should have remembered Sarah right then), and said 'sure'! That very night (I kid you not), I received an e-mail from a business man in a nearby city, saying that he has so many air-mile points, that he has enough for a family of five to fly to Israel. He was asking, "Do you want to use them to return to Israel?"

    I couldn't believe it! But I had given my word before the Lord and besides, things were so dismal for us here that I agreed to pursue the possibility of returning to the Land. This time, David went ahead to scout out a place for us. We had been contacted by a family in the Galilee who said they totally connected with everything I had written and that they believe exactly the same way and that they believe God wants us to join with them. Once again, they knew us only from my writing. They told us all about the village where several Believers lived and it sounded wonderful. David met them in Israel and found a nice home for us to stay and later the children and I joined him. Sounds easy, doesn't it? But that is without mentioning that I had to, on my own, pack, sort, ship, sell, and give away everything we had now accumulated in this three bedroom townhouse (with a basement). Besides still feeling physically unwell and having to care for the three children (toddler, pre-schooler and adolescent), I thought I was seriously going to lose my mind. My mother, trying to help me out by keeping the children and feeling stressed by hearing that I was going to move back to Israel suffered heart palpitations and had to be hospitalized the night before I left. I felt like I was living in hell – and that when I got to Israel, I would murder my husband. I would phone him in Israel and he would be laughing and having coffee with our friends there. What was that God said about not taking revenge? Surely He couldn't mean it in this case!

Up to the Northern Galilee

So we schlepped (hauled) all our luggage and baggage back to Israel in the fall of 2004. When I say we schlepped our baggage, it is not just our physical suitcases that I refer to. As you probably realize, it was our heavy emotional issues that we packed up and lugged back to Israel with us as well.

'Schlepping' (dragging) our 'baggage' back to Israel.

At first, things seemed to be going well. We all loved the Galilee – out of all the places we lived in Israel, this was the most beautiful – green and lush, peaceful and quiet. We lived in a nice, spacious home with an upper floor and a shaded porch where I loved to sit each morning and look out over the mountains and spend time with God. I wrote my most favorite writing from that porch with the lovely view: You are Mine, Chains that Bind, Lesson from the ant…. Even now as I write, I can hear the doves cooing and smell the palm trees and feel the sunshine on the leather couch. But oh, those cracks – we just couldn't keep them hidden. From my writing, the family we connected with in the Galilee expected 'Suzy Spiritual'; but when we couldn't hide our marital and family dysfunction, they were disappointed. Actually, I felt close to the woman and confided many things to her which she later used against me in a horrible, terrible experience that I would never want to repeat. First of all, my son was accused of choking their daughter. To this day, I have no idea what really happened. Then, Timothy stepped on a rake in the back yard and ended up with a terrible shiner – his eye was swollen and black and blue for weeks.

At the Sea of Galilee - Timothy with a 'shiner'.

On top of it all, Avi-ad dove head first one night (don't ask me why) off the bed, knocking his skull against the corner of the door jamb, ending up with a huge purple goose-egg. All this led to accusations of child abuse; and worse yet – they thought it was me![55] Apparently they had overheard some raised voices (a nice way of saying I lose my temper and scream – loudly). We were absolutely devastated. Our marital issues were only getting worse and worse and I felt I could not go on like this any longer. We spent the winter in the Galilee, freezing in our unheated home. We shut off the rest of the house and moved into the kitchen, bathroom and living room, all of us sleeping huddled together on mats under the stairs to stay warm. The house was full of mold and Avi-ad had constant ear infections. I didn't know at that time that he had a sensitivity to mold, but he suffered terribly, his ears running with pus and infection.[56] We knew we were going to have to move again and I just didn't feel like I could bear it. When my parents sent tickets for us to come to Canada for their 50th wedding anniversary celebration, I agreed to come for the summer of 2005. Only the children and I came; David stayed behind, knowing that if he left the country, they would probably never let him back in. He had entered on a tourist visa with his new last name. We had a great summer; it felt so liberating to be free of the continual pain and tension of my troubled marriage. When it came time for me to return at the end of the summer, I just became paralyzed. I couldn't bear the thought of going back to that painful place that I had escaped from. And after so many years, I had no hope of change for the better. It seemed impossible to deal with our issues. Everyone in Israel had advised me to go home, and surround myself with my support network of family and friends. It's not the place

---

55 You can read about this in my article, Accuser of the Brethren, on our website (articles archives)www.voiceforisrael.com

56 You can read about this in Happy Day I & II in the articles archives on our website: www.voiceforisrael.com

to come to the front of the battle when you're already so wounded. And so I phoned David to Israel and told him that I was planning on staying in Canada; that I would not be returning to Israel. I think that in my heart, I was already planning for my escape from the marriage. David returned from Israel and shortly afterwards we separated. It was a devastating time of my life during which I felt that I had lost everything that ever mattered to me.

If we can fast forward a couple of years (no need to describe the same old journey around the same old mountain over and over again). I would take you to the office of a marriage counselor where David sat on one side of the couch and me on the other – crying. "I don't want to work on this anymore. I am in too much pain. I have no hope." I said to her. But she disagreed with me and said, "I think you're wrong. I think you have a mustard seed of hope left." And she was right – I had only a mustard seed of hope that God had brought my husband and I together for His divine purposes - a destiny that involved us being together; one that we could not fulfill individually.

And this is where we live today – sitting on our tiny mustard seed of hope – that somehow God can bring some good out of the shattered pieces of our lives. Just this morning, I read this verse, **"Unto You, O Lord, I bring my life...Show me Your ways, O Lord, teach me Your paths. Guide me in Your truth and faithfulness."** (Psalm 25:1, 4-5)

I would not trade my experiences in Israel for anything – it has been well worth the price in the things the Lord has shown me: from the beautiful sea coast of Netanya, to the 'Territories' of the Shomron (Ariel), to the holy city of Jerusalem, to the dry, desert sands of the Negev, to the lush, fertile Galilee, I have lived and breathed and slept and ate and laughed and wept and had my being filled with the knowledge of God in the Land of Israel. And I have come to know that I don't know; that I really don't have all the answers. Possibly not any of them. This is brokenness. When we finally come to know that He is Adonai (Lord) and we are not! Sometimes we have to go back in order to go forwards; I believe that we had to take a step backwards but that God is, by His grace, going to lead and guide us into a new thing. I just don't know what that is - yet. Sometimes the hand of God seems so hidden; we can't discern what He is doing. How could He possibly be in this pit? In this darkness? In this pain, this abandonment, this betrayal? But like Joseph, thrown into a pit by his brothers, sold into slavery, unjustly imprisoned for years, we need to, we *must come to* a place of being able to say, You know better than I; You know the way...."

All of us are on a journey to Jerusalem – to a city whose foundation is God, a city that cannot be shaken. And so God is shaking everything that can be shaken in our lives. God often mysteriously leads us into His purposes through darkness, obscurity, pain and hardship. It is only through the fiery wilderness, the dry and thirsty land, that we may reach the Promised Land.

Can we see God in the detours of our lives? In the setbacks, the struggles, the failures and disappointments? I love what Peter Scazzero wrote in his book *Emotionally Healthy Spirituality*,

"Every mistake, sin, and detour we take in the journey of life is taken by God and becomes his gift for a future of blessing."

This is my hope and prayer – not just for us but for you in your journey as well, that we could rest in faith in the goodness and love of God – even when our situations go from bad to worse. Do I know where we're going from here?

No, but I know the One who knows and, 'to Him I bring my life." I find myself often disoriented and confused by the unknown territory I walk in. For He is taking me from an external journey to an internal journey of the heart with Him. He is changing us, transforming us from glory to glory. He sometimes uses difficult people and painful circumstances to conform us into the image of His son. I choose to open the door to my future with God and to let the Holy Spirit lead the way. Just as it is the engine that drives the boat and not the wake behind it, I look forward and refuse to let my past, the 'wake' of my life, drive the boat. I have learned some valuable lessons from my past, but the challenge is not to be crippled by them; but to rest in His promises over us, but not demand where, when, or how God in His sovereignty and wisdom, chooses to bring them to pass in our lives.

When we go through such failure and devastation, such brokenness of heart and spirit (as many do), I see that we have only two choices: to become stuck there and die; or to receive forgiveness and move on. Judas became stuck; he betrayed the Lord and later committed suicide. Peter, on the other hand, denied the Lord three times, but received forgiveness and went on to be a founding apostle of the Church, a mighty man of God. We can go through such disillusionment and disappointment that we hit a crisis of faith. I know I certainly did. I remember crying out to God on a daily basis, on my face, crying out for hours and hours and hours for him to rescue me, to heal my marriage, to save me out of this 'living hell' that I felt I was living. Next door, a little tiny kitten had become stuck on the neighbor's roof. They rescued him and I felt it was a sign for me and hope rose up in my heart. Two days later, the kitten died. There are times when it seems like our faith just doesn't 'work' anymore. We don't know where God is anymore. And we don't know how long we will be here in this prison. We begin to wonder if God is some kind of sadist. Does He enjoy

Postscript

watching us suffer? Proverbs says that a man (or woman) 'twists' (perverts) his ways and then his heart rages against God. But God can handle our honest emotions. He uses all of this pressure to refine us, to create in us a clean heart; to renew a steadfast spirit within us; so that we become poor in spirit and free from judgment. He is doing a deep cleansing, not a superficial 'dusting off' in our hearts. We must learn to wait on the Lord and to be content in all circumstances, trusting in Him. God doesn't want us to minimize our grief and our losses; it's okay to admit feeling hurt, angry, sad, forsaken, helpless, weary and empty. God will help us to shed our counterfeit self that tries to pretend everything is okay when it is not; tries to pretend we have the answers for others when we can't even figure out our own life. God will shake us loose from attachments that we 'have to have' to be happy, from idols that we clutch so tightly in our hands. Anything can become an idol, even Israel, when it becomes the focus or our life rather than God.

Will we ever return to Israel? I don't know. Is Israel the true 'Promised Land' as we had once believed? To be honest, I'm not sure. I know that it is a land that is far from the fullness of the promises and blessings of God in many ways. It is a place that is still full of trouble, struggle, strife, and terror. Yes, the exiles of Israel are returning, the desert is blooming, the land is once again fertile, the cities are rebuilt and flourishing, but as a nation, Israel has yet to experience the peace, healing, security and prosperity promised to her in God's eternal Word. I believe Israel will only experience these in their fullness when the Messiah returns. And for this we yearn and wait. Come Adonai Yeshua!

Sarah and Abraham needed to wait for the child of Promise to come forth. His name was Yitzchak which means laughter. Isaac symbolizes the promises of God; their fulfillment in His way and His time brings forth joy. But Sarah became impatient with waiting and used her human strategy to bring forth a 'child of the flesh', Ishmael, born prematurely, resulting in strife and conflict. The book of Galatians makes an interesting reference to Abraham's two sons, one born by a bondwoman (Hagar) according to the flesh, and one by a free woman (Sarah), according to the Spirit. It then goes on to state that these are symbolic of the Old Covenant, symbolized by Hagar, which corresponds to the Jerusalem which is now (present day Jerusalem, established under the Old Covenant) in bondage with her children, and the New Covenant, which is the New Jerusalem, which is free.[57] Just as Ishmael, the child of flesh, persecuted Isaac, the child of promise, so do the religious Jews of today persecute the Messianic Jewish Believers, who walk in the promise of eternity. Is it possible then, given the analogy, that we too have interfered with God's plan and timetable, rushed the promises of God, introduced our human strategies to create an 'Israel of flesh', with its resulting strife and conflict, rather than wait for the Messiah to come and bring us home with Him to the New Jerusalem? I don't know for sure. At one time I thought I did. But I believe it is food for thought – apparently dangerous thought, because when I spoke this in a Messianic congregation they unceremoniously took me off the platform, destroyed the tape and publicly apologized for my presenting of this heretical idea. Israel must never become a 'sacred cow'. Whether she is the true Land of Promise or not, God loves her and will keep covenant with her because He is a God of covenant. The challenge is, will we still love the people of Israel once we have faced the truth of who she is – the good, the bad, and the ugly?

And so I need to say shalom. I do wish I could end this book with a happily ever after conclusion – that my marriage is healed, that we are prospering and in good health, that God has restored all the years that the locust has eaten and

---

57 Galatians 4:21-31

Postscript

we are firmly planted back in the Land....but at present I can't end this way. Perhaps in my next book, I hope. For now, I can only assure you that He who began a good work in me, and in you, will be faithful to complete it – until that day. I think that sometimes we want to be like flying squirrels – leaping from one high tree branch to the other. But God is walking with us and comforting us through the deep, dark valleys as well as leaping joyfully with us across the high mountain tops. Perhaps this is the message, finally, of this book – that one day, by God's grace, we will journey to a New Jerusalem, where He will wipe away every tear from our eyes. There shall be no more death, nor sorrow nor crying. There shall be no more pain, for the former things will have passed away. (Rev. 21:4)

And so wherever you are in your journey, I pray for you the grace and courage to follow God into the unknown places and that He would grant you shalom – peace – along the way.

In the name of Sar Shalom, Prince of Peace, the Messiah, Yeshua who said, "**Do not let your hearts be troubled; you believe in God, believe also in Me. In my Father's house are many mansions...I go to prepare a place for you...I am the way, the truth and the life ; no one comes to the Father but through me.**" (John 14:1-6)

To contact the Author write:

Hannah Nesher, Voice for Israel
Suite #313- 11215 Jasper Ave.
Edmonton, Alberta
T5K 0L5 Canada

www.voiceforisrael.net

Please include your testimony or help received from this book when you write.

Your prayer requests are welcome

Additional Teaching Materials by Hannah Nesher

DVDs

Shalom Morah I (Hebrew for Christians & Hebrew Names of God) 11 DVD set

Shalom Morah II (Hebrew for Christians & Wisdom in the Hebrew Alphabet) 10 DVD set

Exploring the Jewish Roots of the Christian Faith

Unity in the Messiah

Because He Lives

Messianic Jewish Wedding in Jerusalem

There is a God in Israel

Messianic Jewish Passover

Passover Lamb or Easter Ham?

Voice Out of Zion II (Where is Your Brother Jacob?)

Walking Through the Wilderness

Ruth: A Righteous Gentile

Messiah in Chanukah

BOOKS

Grafted in Again
Come Out of Her My People
Messiah Revealed in Purim
Messiah Revealed in the Sabbath
Messiah Revealed in Passover
Messiah Revealed in the Fall Feasts
Messiah Revealed in Chanukah
Kashrut: The Biblical Dietary Laws
Messiah Revealed in Shavuot
You Know My Heart (English booklet)
You Know My Heart (Hebrew booklet)

If you enjoyed this book and would like to learn more, don't miss the companion DVD

THERE IS A GOD IN ISRAEL

Have you ever wondered what is REALLY going on in Israel?

A clear and vibrant presentation from the persepctive of a Messianic Jewish Israeli woman on what the Bible has to say about the Arab-Israeli conflict in the Middle East today.

Great witnessing tool for anyone wanting to encourage others to stand with Israel in these troubled times.

Hannah Nesher, Voice for Israel
Suite #313- 11215 Jasper Ave.
Edmonton, Alberta
T5K 0L5 Canada

www.voiceforisrael.net

www.ingramcontent.com/pod-product-compliance
Lightning Source LLC
LaVergne TN
LVHW051548070426
835507LV00021B/2468